Essential Notes for the MRCPsych

Other Examination Preparation Books Published by Petroc Press:

Obtainable from all good booksellers or, in case of difficulty, from Plymbridge Distributors Limited, Plymbridge House, Estover Road, PLYMOUTH, Devon PL6 7PZ. Tel. 01752-202300, Fax 01752-202333.

Essential Notes for the MRCPsych Part 1

Wai-Ching Leung, MRCP(UK), MRCPsych, MRCPCH, MRCGP
Lecturer in Public Health Medicine, Health Policy and Practice
University of East Anglia, Norwich

and

Kirsty Passmore, MBChB, MRCPsych
Specialist Registrar in Learning Disability
Earls House, Durham

 **PETROC PRESS**

Petroc Press, an imprint of LibraPharm Limited

Distributors
Plymbridge Distributors Limited, Plymbridge House, Estover Road, Plymouth
PL6 7PZ, UK

First edition 2001
Reprinted 2002

Published in the United Kingdom by
 LibraPharm Limited
Gemini House
162 Craven Road
NEWBURY
Berkshire
RG14 5NR
UK

A catalogue record for this book is available from the British Library

ISBN 1 900603 54 3

Typeset by Thomson Press (India) Limited, Chennai
Printed and bound in the United Kingdom by MPG Books Limited,
Victoria Sq., Bodmin, Cornwall PL31 1EG

Contents

Section 4. Psychopharmacology

Section 5. Preparation for Clinical Part of MRCPsych Part 1 Examination

Preface

The MRCPsych Part 1 examination represents the first of many hurdles for the aspiring psychiatrist. The trainee's progress up the career ladder will inevitably be delayed if this examination is not passed early. The Part 1 examination itself consists of two sections. The written section mainly assesses detailed knowledge in psychology, psychopharmacology, psychopathology and clinical psychiatry. From the autumn of 2001, it consists of individual statements, to which candidates must state whether they are true or false. Extending matching items may be introduced in future. Candidates must pass the written section before progressing to the clinical section, and they are allowed four attempts at it. Up until the spring of 2003, it will consist of a long clinical case in which candidates have to perform a full psychiatric assessment on a patient. After the spring of 2003, the clinical section will consist of several observed structured clinical examinations.

Most candidates are under some pressure to sit the examination a year after starting their psychiatric training. Although they will have some clinical experience in psychiatry, they must specifically study for the basic sciences in the syllabus. The syllabus for psychology is especially broad, and few trainees have covered them in their undergraduate years. There are many subsections in the syllabus, and candidates must read textbooks for each subsection in preparing for the examination. The amount candidates have to read through is considerable. It is therefore important for the candidates to have an overview of the syllabus.

This book attempts to summarise the entire MRCPsych Part 1 syllabus and adopts identical sections and subsections to the syllabus, for easy reference. The syllabus does not prescribe detailed topics within descriptive psychopathology. We have also broadly adopted the terms and topics in the authoritative text by Sims with some modification, so that candidates can easily refer to this text for fuller explanations. The clinical section attempts to focus on the clinical part of the examination and provides an overview of common clinical syndromes with attention to clinical features, classification, investigations and aetiology. There is also a section giving advice on how to tackle the clinical section – both for the clinical long case (for examinations before 2003) and the observed structured clinical examination (for examinations during, and after, 2003). This book can be used for three purposes: (1) to provide an initial overview of the syllabus; (2) to ensure that candidates 'can see the woods from the trees' during their study; and (3) as a revision aid to be used during the weeks prior to the examination. However, it does not cover all the topics comprehensively, and it cannot be emphasised too strongly that trainees must not use it as a substitute for reading the main textbooks. A list of useful textbooks is given at the end of this book.

We hope that MRCPsych Part 1 candidates will find this book useful in preparing for their examinations, and we wish them good luck in them!

April, 2001

W.-C. L.

K. P.

Breakdown of content in the MCQ paper

Candidates are required to answer 200 single-statement questions in 90 minutes and to state whether each one is 'true' or 'false'. (N.B.: It is no longer arranged in questions each consisting of five statements.) The college indicated that the breakdown of the types of questions in autumn 2001 will be roughly as shown in the following table. This information may help you to schedule your revision.

	No. of questions in each sub-section	No. of questions in each section
Basic sciences		35
Psychology		
basic	11	
behavioural	14	
social, assessment & neuropsychology	10	
Human development		10
Psychopharmacology		34
general	10	
pharmacokinetics & pharmacodynamics	16	
adverse drug reactions	8	
Psychopathology		64
descriptive	58	
psychodynamic (includes defence mechanisms)	6	
Clinical theory and skills		57
Theory		
aetiology	15	
assessment and classification	15	
Skills		
history taking	11	
mental state	12	
physical/neurological examination	4	
Total		200

1 | Psychology

Basic psychology

Learning theory

Classical conditioning

1. Pavlov: 'Association by frequency of occurrence'.
2. Subject is passive in the learning process.
3. When food (*unconditional stimulus*) is presented to dogs, reflex salivation (*unconditional response*) occurs. However, if the sound of a bell immediately precedes the food on several occasions, the sound of the bell itself (*conditional stimulus*) will cause salivation (*conditional response*).

Operant conditioning

1. Skinner: 'Frequency of response depends on types and timing of reinforcement'.
2. Interaction between the subject and the environment in the learning process.
3. The frequency of response increases with the giving of a reward (i.e. food as a reward for making the correct choice – *positive reinforcement*) or the taking away of something undesirable from the subject (e.g. removing sources of pain – *negative reinforcement*).
4. The frequency of response decreases with the infliction of something undesirable on the subject (e.g. being hit – *punishment*) or the removal of something desirable from the subject (e.g. the deprivation of food – *cost response*).
5. Reinforcement schedules – reinforcement can be dependent on:
   The number of responses – either *fixed ratio* (FR) or *variable ratio* (VR). Fixed ratio means that the ratio of the number of reinforcements to responses are fixed.

The time that has elapsed – either *fixed interval* (FI) or *variable interval* (VI). Fixed interval means that a reinforcement is given after a certain length of time, irrespective of the response.

6. Learning is fastest when the subject sees that the reward is closely linked to the behaviour. Hence, in relation to speed of learning: FR > VR > FI > VI.

7. Extinction – unlearning of a behaviour as a result of the lack of reinforcement after appropriate behaviour.

Table 1. Some differences between classical and operant conditioning

Classical conditioning	Operant conditioning
Occurs automatically as a 'reflex'	Voluntary actions by the subject
Unconditional stimulus is presented irrespective of what the subject does	Reinforcer is presented only if the subject performs certain actions
Unconditional stimulus always occurs before the response	Reinforcer is presented after the subject performs certain actions
Strength of conditioning is measured by magnitude of response or the time taken between stimulus and response	Strength of conditioning is measured by the response rate

Escape and avoid conditioning

Two main forms of negative reinforcement:

Escape conditioning – The subject learns to avoid punishment by performing the 'appropriate' behaviour (e.g. rats learnt to press the appropriate lever to turn off electric shocks; a child learnt to quickly pick up rubbish to avoid punishment, etc.).

Avoid conditioning – The subject learns to avoid punishment by responding appropriately to warning signals (e.g. in a 'shuttle box' in which one of two compartments may be electrified at any one time, rats learnt to avoid electric shocks by quickly moving to the other compartment in response to a warning light in the 'dangerous' compartment; the persistence of phobias in humans; use of antabuse in treating alcoholism).

Two-process theory (Gray, 1975):
1. The subject learns to be afraid through classical conditioning.
2. The subject learns to reduce fear through negative reinforcement.

Punishment

- Although punishment may have strong immediate effects on behaviour, it merely suppresses rather than unlearns the behaviour.
- Punishment suppresses undesirable behaviours more strongly if the desired behaviours are reinforced at the same time.
- It is rarely used clinically for ethical reasons.
- In society, punishment is an effective deterrent only if it is sufficiently aversive, the probability of detection is certain, and occurs soon after the undesired behaviour.
- Criticisms of punishment in society: no new positive behaviours taught; induces a desire for revenge.

Social learning theories

These theories emphasise the importance of observational learning (modelling) and the cognitive factors occurring between a stimulus and response. The cognitive models emphasise the perception of an event in determining the response.

Observational learning (modelling)

- A subject duplicates the actions of another (the model); e.g., children imitate the actions of their parents or TV idols.
- Five processes in modelling (Bandura, 1977):
  1. Paying attention to the modelled events.
  2. Retaining what is learnt from observation.
  3. Retaining in memory (e.g. via rehearsing etc.).
  4. Reproducing a model's behaviour.
  5. Being motivated to do so.
- Factors influencing the likelihood of a model being imitated:
  1. Appropriateness (e.g. children are more likely to imitate aggressive men than aggressive women).
  2. Relevance and similarity (e.g. boys are more likely to imitate aggressive men than girls).
  3. Consistency.

Cognitive models

Tolman's place-learning (or sign-learning) theory – In maze experiments, rats learnt *cognitive maps* which allowed them to know which part of a maze is followed by which other parts. This explains how rats learn to take shortcuts to the food box even if the path is blocked or if the starting points are different.

Insight learning theories (by Gestalt psychologists) – In productive thinking, problems are solved by perceiving new relationships among their elements.

Further concepts on learning processes

Generalisation: Conditional response transfers automatically to stimuli similar to, but different from, the original conditional stimulus. For example, dogs salivate in response to bells of different pitches to original conditional stimulus; animal phobias – patients may become fearful of all animals even though the original conditional stimulus is a particular species of cat.

The opposite of generalisation is *discrimination*. (e.g. dogs salivate only in response to bells of certain pitch.)

Primary and secondary reinforcement

Primary reinforcers – natural reinforcers obviously rewarding in themselves (e.g. food, clothing).

Secondary reinforcers – reinforcers whose properties are derived from their association with the primary reinforcer (e.g. money, which humans are classically conditioned to associate with other primary reinforcers such as food and clothing).

Secondary reinforcement is also used to describe 'secondary gain'. For example, the primary reinforcer for a patient claiming loss of memory after an accident may be the immediate attention he/she receives. The secondary reinforcer is the secondary effect of the possibility of future financial compensation.

Latent learning

In maze experiments, a group of rats were reinforced for finding their way in the maze only after the initial few days. It was found that they rapidly caught up with the group which was reinforced from the very beginning (Tolman and Honzik, 1930). Hence, reinforcement may be important in the performance of learned behaviour, but not the learning itself.

Stimulus preparedness

- Dogs can easily learn to bark or run, but not to wave their tails to avoid shock.
- *Seligman (1970)* – it is very easy for animals to learn actions that are closely related to the survival of their species, but very difficult for them to learn behaviours contrary to their natural tendencies.
- 'Preparedness' in classical and operant conditioning is an inherited characteristic.
- Explains why human phobias are commonly related to animals or potentially dangerous situations (e.g. fear of snakes, spiders, height, closed-in places, etc.).

Explaining clinical features by theories of learning

- *Two-stage model for phobia*
  Aetiology – e.g. in phobias, classical conditioning by association.
  Maintenance – e.g. in phobia, by operant conditioning. Avoidance of phobic objects is negatively reinforced.
- *Learned helplessness model for depression*
- *Alcohol or substance misuse* – explained by operant conditioning. Both positive reinforcement (immediate effects of drugs/alcohol) and negative reinforcement (i.e. avoiding reality).

Clinical applications in behavioural treatments

Habituation – If a stimulus is repeated over a long period of time, the response will decrease. The rate of habituation increases with more frequent and weaker stimuli.

Implosion therapy and flooding – The therapists repeatedly expose patients with phobias to the feared objects (either in imagery or with the real objects). If the fear-evoking stimulus is repeatedly presented without the undesired consequences, the power of the stimulus to evoke fear will be gradually lost (extinction).

Reciprocal inhibition – It is not possible to experience two incompatible emotional states (e.g. anxiety and relaxation) at the same time. This mechanism is used in systematic desensitisation.

Systematic desensitisation – The feared object is *gradually* introduced. Relaxation techniques are taught. Patients are asked to imagine the *feared object when* they are relaxed. Phobias disappear according to *reciprocal inhibition* theory.

Aversive therapy – An example is giving antabuse in the treatment of alcoholism. When taken with alcohol, the drug produces nauseous and unpleasant effects. It works by a combination of classical and operant conditioning. First, the nauseous effects act to replace the pleasant effects of alcohol with unpleasant effects, and classical conditioning between alcohol and fear is established. Second, the unpleasant effects act as negative reinforcer for alcohol taking.

Chaining

- The effects of a reinforcer may be transferred to another neutral stimulus by repeated association. The transferred reinforcement power may then be transferred to any number of other stimuli in a chain: i.e. from B $\rightarrow$ A to C $\rightarrow$ B $\rightarrow$ A to D $\rightarrow$ C $\rightarrow$ B $\rightarrow$ A, etc.;
- chaining may be forward or backward.

Shaping

- A technique to facilitate learning of complex behaviour.
- Sequential reinforcement of behaviours closer and closer to the desired outcomes.
- The desired behaviour is first broken down into a number of small components.
- Each component is reinforced in sequence.
- Used widely by animal trainers.
- Widely used in learning new skills.
- Used in behavioural modification to teach children and adults with learning disabilities.

Cueing

- A stimulus to elicit the conditioned behaviour in operant conditioning; a cue which may trigger the feared object in phobia.
- May be made use of in therapy (e.g., conditioning of the same cue to relaxation).
- Other examples – suggestion of sleepiness or relaxation in hypnosis.

Visual and auditory perception

Gestalt's psychology

According to Gestalt psychologists,

- normal perceptual experience is greater than the sum of its parts,
- the brain interprets the perception in a predictable manner,
- the organisation of the brain responsible for this is determined innately.

Some basic principles: Complex visual patterns are organised according to

- *Similarity* – similar images are grouped irrespective of their position.
- *Proximity* – objects close together are grouped.
- *Continuation* – objects which continue in the same direction are grouped.
- *Common fate* – objects which move together are grouped.
- *Closure* – gaps in a figure are mentally closed to complete the figure.

Figure–ground differentiation

Whether an object is perceived as figure or ground is determined by:

- its familiarity,
- whether it is enclosed – area enclosed is usually seen as the figure,
- its size,
- its symmetry.

In figure–ground reversal, it is capable of being perceived in two different ways because the figure and the ground can be reversed. An example is the Rubin's vase shown below, which can be seen either as a vase or two faces. One stimulus may be associated with more than one perception.

Object constancy

The ability to perceive an object as the same in spite of changes in the information that reaches our eyes:

Size constancy – objects are perceived to be of the same size irrespective of their distance from the observer.

Shape constancy – objects are perceived to be of the same shape irrespective of the angle of observation.

Location constancy – we perceive objects to be stationary when we move our heads.

Brightness constancy – objects are perceived as having approximately equal brightness even when the level of illumination changes greatly.

Colour constancy – familiar objects appear to be roughly of the same colour under very different illumination conditions.

Loudness constancy – the perceived loudness does not change with the distance of the source of sound.

Perceptual set

- The bias or readiness to perceive particular features of a stimulus; i.e. the tendency to notice some aspects of a stimulus and ignore others.
- Both perceiver and stimuli may influence perceptual sets.
- Perceiver factors: immediate need, personality, values, beliefs, cultural background, cognitive style, context and expectations (e.g. the message given below may be read as 'member of the royal college of psychiatrists').

> # Member of the
> # the Royal College
> # of Psychiatrists

Pattern recognition

Template-matching hypothesis – incoming information is compared with templates of previously presented patterns of objects in our long-term memory.

Geometric icon (geon) theory by Biderman – a limited number of simple geometric icons are used to be compared with all complex shapes. Geons can be combined to form more complex ones.

Prototype theories – A smaller number of prototypes (abstract forms representing the basic elements of a set of stimuli) are stored. Similarities between related stimuli are important in pattern recognition

Feature detection theories – Each stimulus pattern is a configuration of elementary features (e.g. vertical or horizontal lines, closed circles etc.). This is supported by visual cortical cells which respond to specific visual patterns.

Perceptual illusions

- Illusions occur when perception does not match the object's physical characteristics.
- Four types of illusions (Gregory, 1983):
  1) Distortions (geometrical illusions) – e.g. which of the horizontal lines is longer?

  2) Ambiguous figures (e.g. Rubin's vase).
  3) Paradoxical figures – 3-dimensional drawings which cannot exist in reality.
  4) Fictions – shape can be determined without real physical contours, but with *subjective* contours.

Theories of visual perception

1) *Gregory's 'constructivist' theory*
   - Perception is a dynamic searching for the best interpretation of available data.
   - This may involve selection of sensory information and filling in missing information with unconscious inferences.
   - Useful to explain geometrical illusions.
   - Cannot explain why different people agree on their perceptual experiences.
2) *Gibson's theory of 'direct perception'*
   - *Optical array* – pattern of light arranged in different time and space.
   - The optical array provides unambiguous information about the objects.
   - Information is in 3 forms:
     a) Optic flow patterns – the patterns of the object's apparent movements.
     b) Texture gradients – important cue to depth.
     c) Affordances – uses of directly perceivable objects for comparison.
   - Difficult to explain illusions using this theory.
3) *Marr's computational theory of vision.* Four bottom-up steps in deriving a representation of object shapes from information in the retinal image:
   - Image description.
   - Primal sketch.

- $2\frac{1}{2}$-D sketch (viewpoint dependent).
- 2-D sketch (viewpoint independent).

Development of visual perception
Is visual perception inborn or the result of experience and learning?

- *Innate theorists* – we are born with the capacity to perceive the world as we do.
- *Empiricists* – our perceptual abilities develop through experience and learning.

Human neonate and infant studies

- Methodologies: Sucking rate, habituation, conditioned head rotation, visually evoked potentials.
- Pupillary and blink reflexes, optokinetic reflex, accommodation and convergence, colour vision are all at adult levels by about 3–4 months.
- Visual acuity of the newborn is poorer than that of the adult (about 6/60) due to anatomical differences between the adult's and the neonate's optical system.
- A 1-month old neonate possesses a degree of 3-D perception.
- Neonates have shape and size constancy at 1–2 months of age.
- Results suggest that many aspects of visual perception are overall innate.

Other approaches

Study of patients who had undergone cataract extraction
- Figural unity does not depend on visual experience, but figural identity and perceptual constancy do.
- Although cross-modal transfer (e.g. from touch to vision) occurs, patients found interpretation of facial expression and judging distances difficult.

Animal experiments on perceptual stimuli deprivation
- Blakemore and Cooper's kittens: Kittens raised in a world with horizontal patterns failed to perceive vertical stimuli and vice versa.
- Two alternative interpretations: (1) Environment determines perception of horizontal/vertical stimuli; (2) cells receptive to different kinds of stimuli are present at birth, but become reorganised if there are no relevant stimuli.

Perceptual distortion and readjustment studies
- Studies investigating how fast people adapt to reversal/inversion of the visual world through special lens.

- Studies assume that the greater/faster the adaptation, the greater the role of learning.
- Generally, people adapt very rapidly on reversion to normal vision.
- Difficult to draw definite conclusions as these adults had already undergone considerable learning before the experiments.

Cross-cultural studies

- These studies compare the perceptions of different cultural groups, usually using visual illusions.
- They assume that differences between cultures are due to social rather than biological factors.
- People of many African cultures had difficulties perceiving depth.

Overall conclusions

Although many aspects of visual perception are inborn, perceptual stimulation and environmental influences are essential for these capacities to develop.

Information processing and attention

Focused attention auditory information processing

- *'The cocktail party phenomenon'* – information processed from only one of several stimuli inputs.
- *Cherry's dichotic listening* – subjects were able to attend to one message only, but they may still make sense of the meaning of the unattended message
- *Single-channel theories* – a filter which allows some information to be passed on for further processing. The rest are discarded (Broadbent).
- However, Treisman found that subjects could sometimes switch their attention to the non-attended ear if meaningful message was presented to the non-attended ear in the middle of a sentence.
- *Treisman's attenuation theory* – the selective filters *attenuate* the non-shadowed message. However, if it includes emotionally relevant stimuli, attention can be switched to the non-shadowed message.
- *Deutsch–Norman theory* – selection occurs only after all information has been analysed at a high level. Pertinent information is attended to. Although it explains why subjects can switch from the attended to the non-attended ear, studies do not support this theory.

Focused attention visual information processing

Treisman's feature-integration theory
- Stage 1 – rapid processing of features of stimuli in the visual environment (e.g. size, colour, shape), no attention required.
- Stage 2 – features of the stimuli are combined to form objects, a slow serial process.
- If attention is not focused or relevant stored knowledge is not available, *illusory conjunctions* (e.g. a green orange) may result.

Duncan and Humphrey's attentional engagement theory – time to detect objects depends on the similarity between the target and distractors.

Divided attention information processing

- 'Dual task performance' – processing of information from more than one stimuli input.
- Performance is easier with:
  1) easy tasks,
  2) practice,
  3) different tasks (e.g. different stimulus modality, different responses, etc.).
- Kahneman (1973) – humans have limited processing capacity. Central processor allocates processing capacity and evaluates demands.
- *Multiple-resource theory* – similar tasks compete for the same modules; dissimilar tasks do not compete.
- *Schneider and Shiffin (1977)* – two types of information processing:
  Automatic – highly practised tasks, non-conscious, fast and accurate, little attentional capacity used, resistant to change (e.g. driving for experienced drivers).
  Controlled – unpractised tasks, conscious effort, slow, limited capacity.
- *Stroop tasks* (e.g. saying aloud colour words on colour cards) – demonstrate competition between automatic and controlled processing system.

Researching information processing in schizophrenia

Stress–vulnerability model (Nucechterlein and Dawson, 1984)
Symptoms depend on the interaction between vulnerability and environmental factors.

- Vulnerability factors: genetic, familial, cognitive.
- Environmental factors:

Stressors – expressed emotion, social stressors, life events, alcohol and drug misuse.
Protectors – social support, medication.

Methods

- Comparing patients who are acutely ill with those in remission.
- Identification of vulnerability factors in patients in remission.
- High risk studies.
- Familial studies – studies of vulnerability factors in relatives of patients with schizophrenia.

Information processing and schizophrenia

Clinical observation
- Krapelin – dysfunction of active attention in schizophrenia.
- McGhie and Chapman – defective attentional filtering mechanism.
  Study findings
- Continuous performance test
  - vigilance task, motor response required (series of letters and digits presented for a fraction of a second);
  - schizophrenic patients in remission and their relatives demonstrated performance deficits;
  - patients with negative symptoms showed more deficits than those with acute psychotic symptoms.

Theories of cognitive deficits in schizophrenia

- Cowan's model (1988)
  - Stimuli → brief sensory store → activate codes in long-term store → enter into consciousness (shift in attention).
  - Central executive – intentionally select stimuli in controlled actions, but not automatic actions.
- Neuchterlein and Subotnik (1998) – initial two phases of perception (entering into sensory store and activation of long-term store) are defective in schizophrenia.
- Hemsley (1993)
  - test reaction time to flanked central letter (e.g. X in AXA);
  - in acute schizophrenia, influence of previously stored memories on current stimulus processing is reduced, leading to sensory overload;
  - leads to negative symptoms as coping strategy for sensory overload;
  - leads to exaggerated awareness of irrelevant stimuli;

- leads in turn to delusions (faulty linking of unrelated stimuli and intrusions from long-term memory) and hallucinations (uninhibited material from long-term memory perceived as real).
- Frith (1992) – in schizophrenia, monitoring system becomes disconnected from intentional acts, hence self-actions and thoughts are perceived as coming from external sources.
- Bentall's social cognition model (1994) – paranoid patients tended to attribute positive events to self (to preserve self-esteem) and negative events to external agencies (symptoms of paranoia).
- These theories might form the basis for cognitive retraining therapy for schizophrenia.

Memory

Multi-store approach to memory

- Three basic steps in information processing:
  - encoding (registration) – sensory input → sensory memory → short-term memory;
  - storage – retaining information in long-term memory (i.e. short-term memory → long-term memory);
  - retrieval – extracting information from long-term memory (i.e. long-term memory → short-term memory → response).
- Optimal conditions for storage:
  - semantic/deep level processing rather than structural/shallow processing,
  - frequent and sophisticated elaboration of material,
  - distinctive material,
  - relevant processing of material,
  - effective organisation of information (e.g. use of referential links such as bizarre and vivid imagery, mnemonic devices).

Memory capacity

- Less than 1% of all sensory information reaches consciousness.
- Of all information which reaches awareness, only 5% is stored in sensory memory.
- Sensory memory retains information only long enough for us to decide whether to process it or not.
- Short-term (i.e. primary) memory – very limited capacity of about 7 ± 2 independent items (chunks) (e.g. 7 ± 2 alphabets, words or numbers).

- Duration of short-term memory – only about 10 seconds without rehearsal; can be held for a long time by constant rehearsal (maintenance rehearsal).
- Long-term (i.e. secondary) memory – almost unlimited capacity.

Chunking

- Capacity of short-term memory limited to 7 ± 2 independent items ('chunks').
- Combining several small pieces of information into larger ones would enlarge short-term memory (e.g. combining letters into words, words into sentences).
- Success depends on a match between incoming information and its representation in long-term memory (e.g. recognition of words or familiar pattern of numbers).

Classification of long-term memory

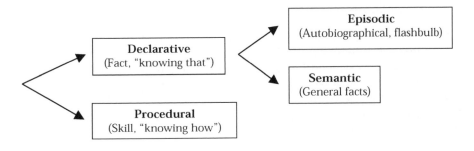

- Semantic memory might be a collection of episodic memories.
- Learning may initially be declarative which cumulates into procedural memory.
- Declarative memory may be selectively impaired in Korsakoff's and other organic amnesia.

The process of forgetting

Decay/trace theory
- structural changes (*engram*) in the brain when learning first occurs; engram ceases to be available unless continually rehearsed;
- decays occurs through disuse;
- explains why forgetting increases over time.

Interference theory
- Forgetting is due to events before or after learning rather than simple passage of time.
- *Retroactive interference* – later learning prevents recall of earlier learning.
- *Proactive interference* – earlier learning prevents recall of later learning.

Proactive interference
- due to failure of retrieval rather than storage;
- e.g. if subjects are told about a change in categories of information before or after the event, proactive interference is less likely.

Displacement theory
- new material pushes out old material in the short-term memory.

Retrieval failure theory
- forgetting due to lack of retrieval cues (e.g. tip-of-the-tongue phenomenon);
- recall improves if the initial context and environmental/psychological state are present.

Emotional factors and retrieval

- *Encoding specificity principle* (Tulving and Thomson, 1973) – recall improves if initial cues at original learning are present during recall.
- *Context-dependent forgetting* – external cues (e.g. environment and context) are important.
- *State-dependent forgetting* – internal cues (e.g. psychological and physiological states) are important; e.g., we are more likely to remember sad events when we are sad.

Distortion, schemata and elaboration

- *Gestalt theory of forgetting* – 'systematic qualitative distortion of the memory trace' towards better and 'more regular' forms.
- *Schemata (Bartlett)* – represent knowledge and experience of the world to help us to interpret incoming unfamiliar information. Act as scripts for the typical events.
- Scripts help us to fill in missing details and allow prediction of immediate future events.
- Also explain distortion of memory and elaboration of past events.

Memory disorders

- *Amnesia* – loss of memory.
- *Organic amnesia* – loss of memory due to brain dysfunction.

- *Korsakoff's amnesia*
  - brain damage caused by chronic alcohol abuse;
  - retrograde amnesia – loss of *episodic* memory before brain injury;
  - anterograde amnesia – loss of ability to form or retain new *episodic* memory.
- *Hysterical amnesia*
  - severe retrograde amnesia;
  - *no* anterograde amnesia.

Thoughts and language

Language development

- Language: A system of rules consisting of phonology (sound), semantics (meaning) and syntax (rules of combining words).
- Language is acquired spontaneously early in childhood without deliberate learning. Humans are born with some knowledge of syntax.
- Language development follows a universal schedule, reflecting maturation of the brain. However, environmental influence is also important.
- Classical conditioning, operant conditioning, behavioural modification and imitation cannot explain the invariant language learning stages and children's creativity of language.
- *Chomsky* – children are born with a *language acquisition device* consisting of *transformational grammar*, which enables a sentence to be transformed from its surface to deep structure and vice versa.

Thought and language

- *Bruner* – language is essential for thought and knowledge to progress beyond the iconic mode to symbolic mode of representation.
- *Sapir–Whorf linguistic relativity hypothesis* – language determines *how* and *what* we think about objects and events (*linguistic determinism*).
- *Bernstein* – middle class children speak in an *elaborated code*; working class children speak in a *restricted code*, and hence are unable to develop their full potential.
- *Piaget* – thought structures language because language 'maps' onto previously learnt structure.
- In children between ages of 2–7, language serves both internal (egocentric speech) and external (conversation) functions. Egocentric speech gradually becomes 'inner speech'.

Concepts, prototypes and cores

- *Concepts* – the psychological representation of the attributes shared by a category of objects. Concepts are formed by abstraction of the attributes shared by the category of objects. 2 functions: to reduce information processing load necessary; to enable prediction.
- *Prototypes (exemplar)* – the most 'typical' of a category of objects. (E.g. for many people, the domestic cat is the prototype of cats. Although lions and tigers are theoretically 'cats', few would regard them as typical of 'cats'.) Prototypes are important in memory and thinking.
- *Core properties of concepts* – the criteria for an object to be regarded as concepts.

Deductive and inductive reasoning

- *Deductive reasoning* – apply general rules to specific problems.
- *Inductive reasoning* – generalise rules from experience and specific examples.

Problem-solving strategies

- *Information-processing approach* – 3 logical stages: define problem, generate possible solutions, evaluate them.
- *Behaviourist theory* – trial and error/accidental success.
- *Gestalt psychologist* – important to understand relations and put structure on a problem.
- Difference between reproductive thinking and productive thinking (involving reorganisation and insight).
- *Expert systems* – computer programs using knowledge in specialist areas, less flexible than human experts.

Generating possible solutions: algorithms and heuristics

Algorithms	Heuristics
Systematic exploration of every possible solution	'Rules of thumb'
Guarantee a solution	Do not guarantee a solution
Time consuming for complex problems	Quicker to reach solution
E.g. flow diagrams, computer programmes	E.g. means-end analysis (working backwards) Analogies (comparison to a previously similar problem)

Personality

Nomothetic and idiographic theories

Nomothetic theories – theories using abstract and general approaches; e.g., theories which attempt to find patterns of behaviour which may allow personalities of all people to be classified. Examples of nomothetic theories:
1. Allport, Cattell, Eynsenck – trait theories.
2. Bandura – modelling.
3. Skinner – operant conditioning.
Idiographic theories – theories relating to individual persons. Examples of idiographic theories:
1. Freud, Jung – psychoanalytic theories.
2. Rogers, Maslow – humanistic theories.
3. Kelly – personal construct theory.

Type approaches

- Hippocrates – 4 temperaments: choleric, sanguine, melancholic, phlegmatic.
- Personality depends on the particular balance of these elements.
- Sheldon – personality development associated with body types: endomorphic, mesomorphic, ectomorphic.

Trait approaches

Allport – 3 types of traits
1. Cardinal – general touching on all aspects of life.
2. Central – general themes which guide our behaviour.
3. Secondary – least important and least general:
   - important to emphasise on the whole personality;
   - current conscious intention is the most important.
Cattell – classify traits using statistical methods called 'factor analysis'.
1. Surface vs source traits:
   - surface traits not permanent and hence less important;
   - 16 source traits – building blocks of personality.
2. Common vs unique traits:
   - common – we all possess to some degree (e.g. introversion).
   - unique – e.g. specific areas of interests.

Eysenck – consider dimensional traits that vary amongst individuals:
1. 3 important dimensions:-
   - extraversion – introversion (orientation towards outwards or inwards);
   - neuroticism-stability (high or low levels of emotion);
   - psychoticism (e.g. impulsiveness, levels of empathy, aggression).

Personal construct theory

- Developed by Kelly.
- A person attempts to understand the world by means of a hypothetical construct.
- We test our constructs against reality. If consistent, we use it again. If inconsistent, we create a new construct.
- If a construct becomes fixed, it becomes our personality.
- Can be used by therapists to help patients to consider alternative constructs.
- Kelly developed Role Construct Repertory Test to help to identify a person's constructs.

Principles underlying psychoanalytic approaches

- Freud: conscious, pre-conscious and unconscious.
- Personality structure: id (pleasure principles), ego (reality principles), superego (internalised ego ideal).
- The three components interact with each other. Defence mechanisms are used to deal with conflict between ego and superego/id
- Psychosexual stages:
  Oral (0–2 yrs).
  Anal (2–3 yrs) – if fixated, either hostile and cruel (anal aggressive) or obsessive (anal retentive).
  Phallic (3–5 yrs) – development of Oedipal conflict or Electra conflict.
  Latency stage (6 yrs–puberty) – sublimation of sexual feelings into other activities.
  Genital stage (adolescence onwards).
- Different approaches used by Jung.

Principles used by humanistic approaches

- Emphasis on
  - individual's subjective experience;
  - self-actualisation;
  - personal values of the persons.

- Maslow
  - Focused on positive side of humans (e.g. happiness, satisfaction)
  - Developed hierarchy of needs (see motivation below).
- Rogers
  - Inborn human actualising tendency to progress towards fulfilment of one's potential.
  - We try to repress experiences which are not consistent with our concept of self.
  - Potential maladjustment occurs if the gap between reality and concept of self becomes too large.
  - Development of self requires *unconditional positive regard*.
  - Full functional individuals have positive self-regard, and the concept of self is flexible.
  - Forms the basis of person-centred therapy.

The interactionalist approach

- An eclectic approach.
- Accepts that behaviour results from interaction between particular dispositions of the person, environmental influences, behavioural tendencies.

Inventories and rating scales

Inventories – a series of questions which attempt to assess personality by the trait/type approach.

Eysenck Personality Questionnaire – measures 4 scales: neuroticism, extraversion, psychoticism, lie or social desirability.

Cattell's 16 personality factor questionnaire (16PF) – 16 basic traits measured in dichotomised scale.

Minnesota Multiphasic Personality Inventory (MMPI) – scores on 10 clinical scales.

- Drawback of inventories: validity of the questions; validity of identifying clusters of factors forming 'dimensions' (usually done by factor analysis).
- Rating scales usually allow subjects to grade their responses (e.g. 5-point or 7-point scale, ranging from 'very strongly agree' to 'very strongly disagree').

Repertory grids

- A grid is drawn with each row representing a construct and each column representing an element.

- Respondent may be asked to consider 3 elements and to identify how one of them is different from the other two. The procedure is repeated.
- Can be based on Kelly's personal construct theory.

Q-sorting

- Assesses personality using a series of statements which a subject sorts (ranks) into categories from 'most typical' to 'least typical' of the subject.
- Focuses on the subjective experience of phenomena (e.g. textual description of events).
- Subjects are asked to place a large number of cards in a grid pattern approximating a normal distribution.
- If the study is repeated with a different group of subjects, an intercorrelational matrix can be constructed and analysed.
- It can be repeated to distinguish between a subject's 'actual self' and 'ideal self'.

Motivation theories

Needs and drives

Needs – states of deprivation.

Drives – purposeful activity produced by needs.

Primary drives – drives arising from intrinsic physiological characteristics (e.g. food, water, avoidance of pain).

Secondary drives – drives arising from social learning processes or their association with primary drives (e.g. affection, comfort, achievement, dominance).

Extrinsic theories and homeostasis

- *Extrinsic motivation* – motivation originating from factors outside the individuals (e.g. punishment, rewards).
- *Homeostasis* – motivation is a part of the mechanism to maintain a state of physiological and psychological equilibrium; e.g. dehydration → feeling of thirst → drive to drink water → motivated to find water and drink → thirst satisfied → restore hydration.

According to extrinsic theories, rewards and punishments are important in motivating others.

Hypothalamic system and satiety

- Stimulation of ventromedial nucleus of hypothalamus → decrease food consumption.
- Stimulus of lateral hypothalamic nuclei (feeding centre) → increase food consumption.
- Dual-centre theory – both inhibitory and excitatory centres exist in the hypothalamus.
- Hypothalamus is affected by hormones, sensory input (e.g. smell, taste), learning.

Intrinsic theories

- *Intrinsic motivation* – behaviours motivated by internal factors (factors perceived to be of value in themselves); e.g. closeness, comfort seeking, social positions, stimulus seeking.
- *Level of arousal* – most volunteers cannot tolerate 'doing nothing' with no external stimulus for more than 2 days.
- *Curiosity* – purposefully seeking selective stimuli the individuals have not encountered before (e.g. pleasure derived from children playing with new toys).

Cognitive consistency

- We have a need to be logical and cognitively consistent.
- Festinger (1957): *cognitive dissonance* – compare two groups of people performing boring tasks: a highly paid group and an unpaid group. Unpaid group considers the task less boring.
- Cognitive dissonance – inconsistency between information from different sources is uncomfortable, and the inconsistency itself motivates the individual to change perception; e.g. a smoker who cannot give up may start to think that continuation of smoking makes no difference as the damage is already done.

Social motivation and need for achievement (n-Ach)

- Social motives dominate our behaviour, which cannot be explained by extrinsic theories.
- McClelland (1953) – We learn from our childhood that certain behaviours lead to fulfilment. We sense a need for achievement (n-Ach), affiliation (n-Aff), and power (n-Power).

- Children with high expectations from their parents tend to have high n-Ach.
- Entrepreneurial behaviour is associated with high n-Ach.
- People with high n-Aff tend to work collaboratively for the benefit of the group.

Necessity to integrate intrinsic and extrinsic theories

- Intrinsic motives may have some homeostatic functions; e.g. cognitive consistency and social learning may lead to homeostasis.
- Curiosity may be a homeostatic mechanism as prolonged sensory deprivation may lead to neurological impairment.

Maslow's hierarchy of needs

- An attempt to integrate various theories.
- We have different levels of needs.
- We need to satisfy needs at one level before moving to the next.
- *Problems with the theory*: some can achieve self-actualisation without fulfilling all the needs above it; some needs appear absent in individuals.

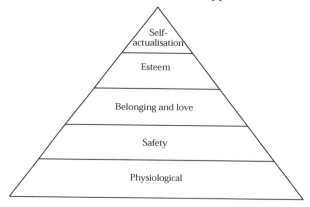

Emotion

Components and theories of emotional response

- Four components of emotional response: subjective feelings, cognitive processes, physiological arousal, behavioural reactions.
- *James–Lange Theory* – Perception of events → bodily changes (visceral and skeletal) → interpreted by cerebral cortex as emotion.
- *Cannon–Bard Theory*

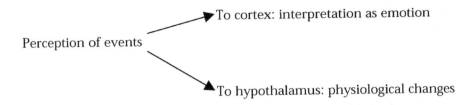

Perception of events

To cortex: interpretation as emotion

To hypothalamus: physiological changes

Critical appraisal of James–Lange and Canon–Bard theories

James–Lange theory

- Each emotion would need to be represented by a separate pattern of bodily changes.
- Subjects injected with adrenaline described physical changes with no emotional overtones.
- Study results on the ability of patients with spinal cord damage to experience the same intensity of emotion are conflicting.

Canon–Bard theory

Supporting evidence:
- Stimulation of specific areas of the brain produces emotion in animals.
- Central brain mechanisms (e.g. endorphins) may be linked to emotion.

Conflicting evidence:
- Drug effects on emotion vary enormously amongst individuals.
- Schachter and Singer experiments (1962):
  1. adrenaline causes subjects' emotion only if subjects were not told of the physiological effects
  2. for subjects not told of the physiological effects, exact emotion was significantly affected by confederate's behaviour.

Schachter and Singer's cognitive labelling theory

- We label emotions from our perception of bodily changes.
- Labelling is a cognitive process significantly affected by our beliefs (e.g. if we believe we have reasons to be happy, the bodily changes will be interpreted as happiness, etc.).

Appraisal theories

- Emotion and stress are products of initial events, accompanying bodily changes and our personal interpretation and evaluation of events.

- Primary appraisal – assessment of the immediate personal implications of an event.
- Secondary appraisal – evaluation of our own coping strategies.
- Appraisal is strongly affected by our pre-existing knowledge and beliefs (e.g. irrational negative appraisals are common in depression).

Emotions and performance
Spielberger's state-trait model of anxiety on performance

- A person's immediate anxiety state depends on both trait anxiety and external stressor (e.g. previous experience of failure).
- A person's immediate anxiety state determines information-processing ability and performance.

Yerkes–Dodson law

- States of moderate arousal are optimal for performance.
- Optimal level of arousal increases for more difficult tasks.

Critique

Effects of stressors on performance depend on the level of information processing required by the task.

Stress

Physiological aspects

- *Stress* – a pattern of negative physiological and psychological responses to perceived threats to individual's well-being.
- Involves an interaction between external stressors and the physiological/ psychological responses to them.

Physiological theories

Salye's general adaptation syndrome – 3 stages: alarm, resistance and exhaustion.
- *Alarm – hypothalamic responses*
  - release corticotrophin hormone which stimulates the release of ACTH from the pituitary and corticosteroids in the adrenal gland;
  - activate the sympathetic nervous system to release adrenaline and noradrenaline.

- *Resistance stage*: Corticosteroids and sympathetic nervous system activity remain high. However, the body's resources are used up faster than they are replaced.
- *Exhaustion stage*: Body's resources are lost. Collapse and stress-related illness may occur.
  Arousal theory:
- Arousal – states of generalised physiological responses (often measured by EEG).
- Moderate arousal is best.

Psychological aspects

- Effects on psychological aspects may be beneficial initially, but become harmful if excessive.
- Cognitive appraisal important – see 'Emotion' above.
- Consequences of stress: emotional discomfort, impairment of social functioning, physical and psychological health problems, disrupted attention and performance.

Situational factors

- Potential situational stress factors: life events, daily hassles, conflict.
- Life events appear to be significantly associated with physical diseases (e.g. heart diseases, cancer) in several studies.
- Longitudinal studies are essential to evaluate whether these effects were real.
- Expressed emotion (level of hostility and criticism) is associated with poorer prognosis for psychiatric patients, especially schizophrenia.

Type A and B behaviour

- Friedman and Rosenman – study of 39–59-year-old initially healthy men regarding eating habits and ways of coping with stressful conditions.
- 2 equal groups:
  Type A – ambitious, competitive, easily angered, hard-working, expect perfection from themselves and from others.
  Type B – relaxed, understanding, forgiving, not easily angered.
- Initially, type A personality was thought to be more likely to have myocardial infarction or angina.
- However, type A personality might be a response to, rather than a cause of, physiological reactivity.

- Some aspects of type A behaviour (e.g. hostility, aggressiveness) may be more important than others.

Coping mechanisms

Task (problem) focused – deal directly with external demand.

Emotion focused – deal by changing internal feeling and thoughts about the problem.

Avoidance – attempt to avoid the problem by engaging in alternative activities.

Seeking social support – often used in conjunction with problem focused approach.

Locus of control

- Internal locus of control – those who take responsibility for their own actions and perceive themselves to have control over their own destiny.
- External locus of control – those who perceive control as residing outside themselves and attribute their success and failure to others.
- Those with internal locus of control cope better.
- Occupations which allow individuals to make decisions (e.g. executives) appear to have less risk of coronary heart disease.

Learned helplessness and learned resourcefulness

- Learned helplessness (Seligman) – helplessness is a learned state due to exposure to situations in which there is no possibility of escape or avoidance.
- Animal model – animals are shocked irrespective of their actions.
- At the end of experiments, animals would not escape even when it was possible.
- Learned resourcefulness – learned state to be ready to cope with external stressors.

States and levels of awareness

Unconsciousness

Three possible meanings:

- as in coma caused by organic brain disease (used in descriptive psychopathology);
- as in deep sleep;
- as in repression of memories too painful to acknowledge (used in analytic psychopathology).

Dimensions of consciousness

Vigilance–drowsiness – the ability to stay alert deliberately when otherwise one might become drowsy or asleep.
Lucidity–clouding – the level of awareness of internal and external stimuli.
Consciousness of self – the ability to experience, and an awareness of self.

Level of consciousness

- *Heightened consciousness.*
- *Normal consciousness.*
- *Clouding of consciousness* – impairment of consciousness, slight drowsiness, difficulty with concentration and attention.
- *Drowsiness* – tendency to drift into unconsciousness, but kept awake with constant stimuli; subjective sleepiness; slurred speech, slow actions; reduced muscle tone.
- *Sopor* – mostly unconsciousness, but temporarily kept awake by strong stimuli.
- *Coma* – unarousable even with strong stimuli.

Disturbed attention, concentration and orientation

Attention, concentration and orientation are important tests of cognitive functions.

Attention
- Voluntary or involuntary focusing of consciousness on a task.
- May be reduced
  normally – sleep, hypnotic state, tiredness, boredom;
  abnormally – organic states (e.g. brain injury, drugs or alcohol, metabolic disturbance, etc.), in mania or dissociation.
- May be *narrowed* in depression (by being preoccupied with morbid themes).

Concentration
- The maintenance of focusing of consciousness on the task.
- May be reduced in organic state, in mania (due to increased distractibility) or in psychosis (due to having to concentrate on listening to voices).

Orientation
- The awareness of one's setting in terms of time, place and person.
- Disorientation in time occurs earliest – ranges from inaccuracy by more than an hour for the time of day to incorrect day of the week, the month, or even the year.

- Disorientation in place occurs next, followed by failure to identify other persons.
- Failure to know one's own name occurs in the most advanced stage.

Sleep stages

- Within the first hour, sleep progresses from stage 1 to stage 4.
- Slow wave sleep (SWS) – stages 3 and 4.
- After the first hour, slow wave sleep alternates with rapid eye movement sleep (REM sleep).
- REM sleep increases in length from about 5 min initially to about 45 min at the end of the night and occurs periodically about every $1\frac{1}{2}$ hours.

Stage 1
- May alternate with wakefulness.
- Low voltage slow activity waves (2–7 Hz).
- Slow eye movements.

Stage 2
- Sleep spindle bursts (13–15 Hz).
- Theta waves.
- K-complexes.
- Lower slow waves with frequency < 2 Hz.

Stage 3
- Usually occurs within half an hour from sleep.
- High-amplitude *slow waves* occupy about 35–50% of the period.

Stage 4
- > 50% slow waves.

Variation of sleep stages

- About 30% sleep is made up in 'catch-up' sleep: most stage 4 sleep and about 50% of REMS is made up.
- REMS – more easily terminated than other stages.
- Neonates sleep for 16 hours a day, 75% of which is REMS.
- Older people – more time with stage 1 sleep.

Sleep disorders

Sleep is different from reduced consciousness (as in coma) in that

1) arousal mechanisms, though temporarily suspended, can be readily brought back;
2) sense of time is preserved to some degree during sleep.

Dreaming

- More frequent and vivid during REM sleep – hence usually later at night.
- Dreams are mostly forgotten and long dreams are unlikely to be remembered.
- Activation–synthesis model of dreaming:
  - memories activated during sleep, followed by cognitive synthesis of dream plot;
  - brain is active, but internal and external realities cannot be distinguished;
  - dream is not transferred to long-term memory.
- Freud
  - unconscious thoughts (e.g. wishes) transformed into more acceptable symbols;
  - symbols are organised to form a coherent dream;
  - dreams can be decoded by free association.
- It is unclear whether dreams can add to what we already know consciously.

Parasomnias

Narcolepsy

- Hypersomnia.
- Cataplexy.
- Sleep paralysis.
- Hypnagogic or hypnopompic hallucinations.

Somnambulism (sleepwalking)

- Usually occurs in children, especially boys.
- Occurs during deep sleep (stage 3 and 4).
- Usually occurs in the first third of nocturnal sleep.
- The subject may walk about or leave the bedroom, but have a blank, staring face with little awareness of the environment.
- Difficult to be woken up during the episode.
- Usually returns to bed unaided.
- Risk of injury if the subject leaves the house unattended.
- No recollection of the episode the next morning.
- Usually no underlying organic disorders.

Sleep terrors

- Usually occur in the first third of nocturnal sleep.
- Episodes of waking up from sleep with intense terror and panic.

- Associated with vocalisation, body motility, and sympathetic discharge.
- Lasts up to 10 minutes.
- Subject usually unresponsive to the attempt by others to comfort.

Nightmare
- Dreams associated with fear.
- More likely with vivid dreams.
- Usually occurs late at night during REM sleep.

Bio-rhythms

Circadian rhythms
- Consistent cyclical variations over a period of about 24 hours.
- Occur with most bodily functions:- heart and breathing rates, body temperature, hormonal levels, etc.
- Rhythm persists for some time even if
  - activity pattern is reversed (hence jet lag);
  - external cues about the time of the day are absent.
- *Internal clocks* – suprachiasmatic nuclei in hypothalamus receives information from retina, determines light–dark cycles.
- *Interval clocks* – determine duration. Reside in striatum and substriata nigra.

Other rhythms
- *Infradian rhythms* – those longer than a day, e.g. menstruation.
- *Diurnal rhythms* – rhythms during the waking day, either morning or evening types (e.g. in alertness, cognitive ability).

Effects of sleep deprivation

- Increased desire to sleep.
- From day 2 – impaired attention and information processing ability.
- From day 3 to 4 – micro-sleep occurs.
- From day 6 – 'sleep deprivation psychosis'; perceptual disorders, hallucinations and delusions may occur.
- Recovery sleep – usually shorter than the period of deprivation.
- Little evidence of adverse physical harm.

Hypnosis and suggestibility

- *Hypnosis* – a state of relaxation induced by hypnotist's suggestions.
- Some therapies may be easier to carry out during this state of relaxation.
- During hypnosis, the subject's attention focus is voluntarily narrowed to the suggestions of the hypnotist.

- The subject suspends attempts at control and reality testing.
- Can be abruptly terminated if emergency occurs or suggestion is strongly against the subject's moral value.
- *Suggestibility* – the condition of being readily responsive to opinion from others, when no force, argument, or coercion is used.
- Some subjects are more suggestible than others, although most willing subjects can be hypnotised.
- Depth of hypnosis may vary from hypnoidal state, via light and medium hypnosis, to somnambulism.

Other plausible theories of the mechanisms of hypnosis

Dissociation theory – volition, control and behaviour are dissociated from the normal awareness. Dissociation is particularly characteristic in a hypnotic trance.

Conditioning theory – hypnosis is caused by association of certain behaviour with a certain stimulus. Partially useful in explaining post-hypnotic suggestions.

Meditation

- A state of extended reflection or contemplation.
- Subjective feelings of relaxation.
- Techniques usually acquired by instruction and practice.
- EEG pattern – generally slow waves.
- Reduced oxygen consumption and energy expenditure.

Trance

- Temporary loss of:
  - sense of personal identity;
  - full awareness of surroundings.
- Subject may act as if taken over by another personality.
- Most likely to be a form of dissociation.
- May occur under hypnosis or intense religious devotion.

Social psychology

It is the study of how the actual or imagined presence of others may influence the thought, feeling and behaviour of the individual.

Attitudes

Some definitions

- Internal affective orientation which explains the actions of a person.
- Mental state of readiness influencing an individual's responses.

Components

- *Cognitive* – belief.
- *Affective* – feeling.
- *Behavioural* – pattern of behaviour, often a function of both cognitive and affective elements.
- *Evaluative*
- *Conative* – disposition for action.

Measurement

Thurlstone – method of equally appearing intervals:

1. Researchers devise a large number of attitude statements of varying positivity towards the relative attitude.
2. A group of judges classify the attitude statements into 11 categories according to how positive they perceive them to be. Only statements with good agreement are used.
3. Respondents are asked whether they agree with each of the statements.
4. The total number of the 'agree' statement scores are averaged.
5. The score should be an interval scale (i.e. difference between 2 and 4 is the same as difference between 4 and 6).

Likert scale

- A list of attitude statements are made up, and respondents are asked to rate how far they agree with the statements (from 'strongly agree' to 'strongly disagree', often with 5 or 7 categories).
- Simpler than Thurlstone scale.
- Score is *not* in interval scale.

Semantic differential scales

- Words have 2 meanings: dictionary meaning (semantic or denotative), or someone's feeling about the word (connotative).
- Attitude can be measured by assessing the connotative meaning (e.g. how 'good' or 'bad' a word is).

- 3 connotative components: evaluation (good/bad), potency (strong/weak), activity (fast/slow).

Attitude change and persuasive communication

- Attitudes are generally resistant to change.
- Explained by cognitive consistency and avoidance of dissonance as strong human motivation.
- 2 basic methods:
  Incentive-based – use of rewards and punishment; based on conditioning theory, concentration on behaviour.
  Argument-based – aim to change knowledge, attitude and behaviour.
- Hovland 'message learning approach' – 3 stages:
  – attention to message,
  – comprehension of message,
  – acceptance of message.
- 4 factors determining strength of a message
  source – attractiveness, authority and credibility of communicator;
  message – comprehensibility;
  receiver – intelligence and level of education;
  channel – written, face-to-face, telephone, e-mail, etc.
- Elaboration-likelihood model – strength of message increases with how deeply the recipient thinks about the matter.
- Heuristic-systematic model – 2 reasons for acceptance of message, systematic processing (i.e. focusing on the issue itself) or heuristic (i.e. using rules of thumb).
- People's information processing may be affected by:
  accuracy motivation – prefers unbiased information;
  defence motivation – prefers opinions which are psychologically comfortable to them;
  impression motivation – attitudes which are accepted socially.

Cognitive consistency and dissonance

- We feel uncomfortable about inconsistencies between the information we receive from various sources and our belief.
- Hence, psychological mechanisms are used to resolve such inconsistencies, e.g.
  – distorting or disbelieving information from one source;
  – disbelieving that the two pieces of information are related.
- Cognitive dissonance theory (Festinger)

- Compared to subjects who were paid $20 for performing tedious tasks, those who received $1 for the same tasks were more likely to lie to others that the tasks were interesting.
- *Explanation*: Subjects who were paid $20 justified their participation by the financial gain. Those paid $1 resolved their dissonance by changing their cognition that the tasks were interesting.
- This accounts for the 'sour grapes' phenomenon.
- Explains why health education often does not result in behavioural changes.

Attitude–behaviour relationship

- *La Pieere (1934) – separation of attitude and behaviour*: In an anti-Chinese climate in USA, Chinese visitors at hotels and restaurants were welcomed although anti-Chinese attitudes were found in written questionnaires to the managers of hotels and restaurants.
- Theory of reasoned action (Fisbein and Ajzen, 1975):

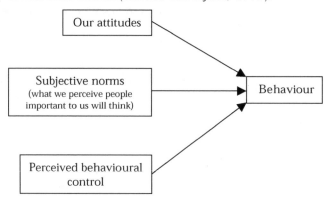

- *Festinger and Carlsmith* – behaviour may determine our attitude.

Self-psychology

Self and its dimensions

- James (1890)
  'I' – the 'inner' or 'perceiving' self, the witness to events.
  'me' – the social self, roles which I play, which consist of: the spiritual self, the material self, the social self and the bodily self.

- Argyle (1994) – 4 dimensions of self:
  Self-image – the 'imagined self; what the self supposes itself to be. May be different from the 'real self'. Contains the core (e.g. gender, identity) and the roles played by the individual.
  Self-esteem – the value which one attaches to oneself. It may be absolute or relative to others. It may change with one's mood state (e.g. low in depression).
  Ego-self – what one would ideally like to be.
  Integration of the self – the consistency of the various dimensions of the self.
- Self-concept – one's full *descriptive* concept of oneself. Different from self-esteem as self-concept does not involve value judgement.

Self-recognition and personal identity

- Lewis and Brooks-Gunn (1979)
  - observation of children in front of a mirror;
  - self-recognition starts from 9 months and steadily develops until about 3 years;
  - children are able to recognise themselves on video from about 15 months.
- Personal identity – our personal characteristics and attributes which make us unique.

Interpersonal issues

Personal perception

- Cook (1971) – study of how people react and respond to others in thought, feeling and action.
- *Intuition theories* hold that perceptions of other people are
  - Intuitive; hence people are 'born with' ability to judge others;
  - global;
  - immediate or direct.
- *Inference theories* hold that perceptions of people come about by
  - a general principle that a first attribute is linked to a second;
  - noting that a particular person has a first attribute;
  - deducing that the person has a second attribute.

Affiliation

- The basic need for the company of others.

- 3 possible functions:
  - to avoid loneliness;
  - to gain the attention of others;
  - to reduce anxiety (e.g. people are more likely to be with others when anxious).

Friendship

- Argyle (1994) – 3 sources of satisfaction;
  - sharing interests;
  - emotional support;
  - instrumental rewards.
- Developed from earlier affiliation needs.

Naive psychology

- Not only psychologists, but all humans try to understand the way they think, feel and behave.
- Foundations for attribution theory.

Attribution theory

- Attribution – imputing a characteristic (e.g. personality trait, motive, emotional state) to a person.
- Attribution may be
  - dispositional (internal – someone has a tendency to do something);
  - situational (external – related to the immediate environment).
- Attribution theory – an approach to how people explain human behaviour.
- Kelly's covariation model – 3 types of information to make causal attributions:
  - consensus (e.g. does everyone say A is good?);
  - consistency (Do they say so all the time?);
  - distinctiveness (Do they say the same thing about other people?).
- 3 factors to infer whether observed behaviour is due to the stable quality of the observed
  - under free choice (rather than coerced);
  - when it is unexpected in the social context;
  - if only one particular outcome is achieved.

Primary (fundamental) attribution error
In interpreting the behaviour of others, the tendency to

- overestimate the influence of internal trait and;
- underestimate external environmental influence.

Social behaviour in social interactions
Most people possess certain social skills, such as

- verbal communication – initiation, turn-taking, maintenance of conversations;
- non-verbal communications – level of eye contact, tone of voice;
- respecting others' personal space.

Some people with mental health difficulties appear to be lacking in some of these skills. Social skills training may be helpful in patients with neuroses, but not in those with psychosis or genetic disorders.

Theory of mind

- An ability to infer mental states and intention in oneself and in others.
- Helps to understand communicative and linguistic development in infants and toddlers.
- 3-year-olds do not appear to understand others' mistaken belief, 4-year-olds do.
- Many children with pervasive developmental disorders (e.g. autism) have deficits in 'theory of mind' abilities.
- In autism, it is still debated whether the observed impairment represents an artefact in measurement, and if real, whether it causes the main symptoms observed.
- Preverbal cognition is important for language acquisition.
- Important links between the development of 'theory of mind' and communicative competence.

Elemental linguistics as applied to interpersonal communication

Verbal communications – both what and how words are uttered.

Linguistics – study of origins, evolution and structure of a language.

Paralinguistics – study of aspects of verbal communication not purely linguistic (e.g. tone of voice, pace, emphasis, etc.). Emphasis on how, rather than what, words are uttered.

Chomsky – language ability is largely determined by genetics and all languages share the same 'universal grammar'. Hence, language gives valuable information on the structure of the brain and mental processes.

Leadership, power and groups

Leadership

- Leadership – the exercise of authority and influence within a social group to achieve specific goals.
- Leadership style:
  - autocratic;
  - democratic – probably optimal;
  - laissez-faire.
- 2 requirements for leadership effectiveness:
  - task (getting the job done);
  - relationship (cultivating a good working atmosphere in the group).
- 3 situational variables determining situational control:
  - good quality of leader–member relationship;
  - structured task structure;
  - high position, power of the leader.
- Fiedler's contingency model of leadership effectiveness:
  - good fit between a leader's style and the requirements of the situation; i.e. a task-oriented leader is optimal if the situation is highly controlled or highly uncontrolled;
  - relationship-oriented leader is optimal if the situation is of medium level of control.

Five types of social power

- *Legitimate* – formal authority (e.g. a manager's direct authority over subordinates).
- *Reward-oriented* – capacity to reward (e.g. performance related pay).
- *Coercive* – administer or threaten punishment (e.g. of dismissal or demotion).
- *Information-oriented (expert)* – leader viewed as possessing extra information.
- *Referent (charismatic)* – personal qualities (e.g. charm, persuasion).

Power and obedience

- Tendency of humans to obey authority as demonstrated by Milgram's experiments.
- Milgram's experiments:
  - participants were assigned to be 'teachers' of stooges who pretended to be electrically shocked by the participants if they failed to learn.

- In fact the stooges received no shock, although the participants believed they did.
- About 65% of participants were willing to give up to lethal level of electric shock.
- Factors decreasing obedience:
  - increasing proximity;
  - increasing touch proximity;
  - peer rebellion;
  - remote authority (e.g. authority by telephone rather than face-to-face);
  - peer-delivered punishment;
  - participants told they are responsible for the consequences.

Influences in a small group
The considerable tendency to conform by group pressure is shown by:

- Sherif (1935)
  - using a visual illusion whereby a non-moving beam of light viewed in total darkness appears to move;
  - when asked in groups, individuals usually converge to the group norms, which they retain when tested individually afterwards.
- Asch (1952)
  - when other members of the group were stooges who deliberately gave the wrong answers, subjects also tended to agree with this wrong answer;
  - conformity increases with larger group size, unanimity, more difficult tasks, less ambiguity and familiarity.
  - 'minority' stooges can also be influential if they show autonomy, coherence, commitment to a particular point of view, and a good balance between flexibility and rigidity.

Influences in a crowd and mob

Crowd – collection of people around some common focus of attention.
Mob – Unified crowd with aggressive intent.
- *Contagion theory* – individuals are simply attracted by the mood of the crowd.
- *Convergence theory* – as in a small group, see above.
- *Emergent norm theory* – carefully orchestrated behaviour with clear purposes.
- *Polarisation and groupthink.*

Polarisation and groupthink

Polarisation – tendency of a group to adjust opinions so that they are at an extreme end of a bipolar continuum.

Groupthink – tendency of a group to reach decisions which are extreme and usually unwise. Typical characteristics:
- highly cohesive group with similar views;
- group members ignore inconsistent information;
- disapproval against any group member who disagrees;
- decision may appear to be unanimous.

De-individuation

- The loss of one's sense of individuality; e.g. in mobs when the individual's choice is submerged in mob action.
- E.g. Zimbardo's Stanford University Prison Study:
  - students volunteered to be either prisoners or guards to enact prison life;
  - the 'guards' were so absorbed in their roles that they took extreme actions;
  - de-individuation with loss of rationality may occur behind the role played.

Intergroup behaviour

Prejudice, stereotypes, discrimination, intergroup hostility

- To 'prejudge' someone on the basis of their membership of a particular group.
- Resistant to reversal when exposed to contradictory knowledge.
- May be either positive or negative (although often used in the negative sense).
- 3 elements:
  - cognitive (stereotyped beliefs);
  - affective (negative feelings);
  - behavioural (discrimination).
- Stereotype is
  - the general tendency to place a person in categories according to some easily identifiable characteristic (e.g. sex, race, age) and attribute

qualities believed to be typical of members of that category to the person;
- not necessarily abnormal; may merely reflect people's need to organise information in everyday life.
• Discrimination
  - is implementing prejudicial beliefs;
  - may be due to fear of rejection by other group members.
• Intergroup hostility
  - Tajfel et al. – 'minimal group paradigm': merely belonging to a particular group and being aware of another group's existence is sufficient.
  - Social categorisation theory – division of the world into us ('ingroup') and them ('outgroup').
  - A general tendency to evaluate 'ingroup' members as being more alike in attitudes, behaviour and appearance, and 'outgroup' members as less alike.

Social identity and group membership
Tajfel and Turner (1986) – Social identity theory:

• We strive to achieve and maintain a positive self-image.
• 2 components of self-image: personal identity and social identity.
• Social identity – a sense of what we are like, derived from the groups to which we belong.
• Group membership provides people with a positive self-image and a sense of belonging in the social world.
• It may explain confirmatory bias (we prefer evidence which confirms our beliefs) and self-fulfilling prophecies (what we expect of others determines their behaviour to some extent).

Aggression

Definitions and types

• Involves some physical or symbolic behaviour intended to harm another person.
• *Instrumental aggression* – goal is to achieve something other than aggression (e.g. bank robbery, hijacking).
• *Hostile (affective) aggression* – goal is to harm or hurt others.

Theories

Social learning theory

- Observational learning – observing others who serve as models for behaviour.
- Bandura – showed experimentally (using Bobo doll) that children can observe and learn aggression.
- A child's aggressive tendency was strengthened if the aggressive model was rewarded (vicarious reinforcement).
- Main sources for modelling: family, teachers, friends, mass media.

Operant conditioning

- Walters and Brown (1963) – children rewarded irregularly are slower to stop than children rewarded continuously, when reward is withdrawn.
- In everyday life, aggressive behaviour may be irregularly rewarded. This may explain why aggressive behaviour is common.

Ethology

- The use of natural environment and evolution to study human behaviour.
- Lorenz (1966)
  - explained aggression in terms of instincts;
  - ritualisation of aggressive behaviour in animals – with losers displaying 'appeasement behaviour' to show acceptance of defeat;
  - in humans, appeasement behaviour is often not effective.

Frustration–aggression hypothesis
Dollard et al. (1939):

- Frustration – something which hinders a goal achievement.
- Frustration leads instinctively to an aggressive drive.
- Catharsis – aggression helps to lower the aggressive drive.
- Displacement – aggression may be directed to a more distant object.

Arousal

Berkowitz's cue-arousal theory
- Frustration + readiness for aggression + environmental cues → aggression.

Zillman's excitation-transfer theory
- Arousal from one source (e.g. physical exercise) can be transferred to and energise some other response (e.g. verbally insulted).
- Aggression may be increased if the subject incorrectly attributes the original source of arousal.

The influence of television and other media

Bandura – children can acquire aggressive behaviour via TV (symbolic) models.

Correlational studies – amount of television watched correlated with aggressive behaviour; However, cause and effect uncertain.

Longitudinal studies – conflicting results on the relationship between exposure to TV violence and aggression.

Family and social backgrounds of aggressive individuals

- Aggressive children tend to commit criminal offences in adulthood – for both violent and non-violent crimes.
- Antisocial behaviour is much commoner in men than in women.
- Aetiological factors are not entirely clear, but may include: harsh and inconsistent discipline in childhood, absence of positive parenting.

Altruism and related issues

Altruism and helping relationships

- Ethology – some species of birds give out alarm signals to other birds which may place themselves under danger. Possible selective advantage of altruism. Selfish-gene hypothesis may be applied.
- Latane and Darley 5-step decision model of bystander intervention:
  1. Noticing the event.
  2. Defining the event as an emergency – we are less likely to define a situation as dangerous if others are around (*pluralistic ignorance*).
  3. Assuming personal responsibility. We are
     - less likely to act in the presence of others (*diffusion of responsibility*, inverse law of helping behaviour);
     - more likely to help if we believe we have the competence.
  4. Deciding what type of help is appropriate.
  5. Implementation – evaluate the balance of time, risks and rewards involved.

Social exchange theory

- Costs of social relations – time, emotional energy, commitment, etc.
- Homans (1974) – we engage in social relationship if rewards > costs.
- Clary and Snyder (1991) – motivation for volunteering to help in situations where material rewards are unlikely include:
  human understanding – to acquire people skills,
  career prospects – increasing number of contacts and experience,
  guilt reduction,
  social approval – to be part of a group,
  self-esteem enhancement,
  humanitarian values – showing concerns for others.

Interpersonal co-operation

- Usually occurs when a shared goal cannot be achieved by one individual alone, but needs the effort of a group.
- Prisoner's dilemma. (One of many versions: 2 suspects were arrested for conspiracy to murder and put in different cells. If both deny, both would be acquitted. If both admitted conspiracy to murder, both would be imprisoned for 10 years. If one admitted but the other denied, the person who admitted would be given immunity from prosecution and he would give evidence against the other, who would be imprisoned for life.) From a combined viewpoint, the best result would be if both deny. From an individual viewpoint, the best result would be to admit irrespective of what the other person does.
- Experimental study using prisoner's dilemma found co-operation is more likely with:
  - smaller number of people,
  - potentially less risk and costs, and higher benefits to individuals,
  - previous familiarity with the other persons,
  - increased communication between individuals,
  - higher chance of future dealings (rather than the one-off dealing).

Neuropsychology

Memory

- Limbic system (studied by electrostimulation studies) – a memory circuit consisting of

- hippocampus,
- amygdala (in temporal lobes),
- parts of thalamus and hypothalamus.
- Damage to the hippocampus caused in a patient 'HM' who underwent neurosurgery for temporal lobe epilepsy:
  - some retrograde amnesia (loss of memories of events prior to neurosurgery);
  - severe anterograde amnesia.
- Korsakoff's syndrome, profound anterograde amnesia, follows Wernicke's encephalopathy with damage to mamillary body and thalamus.
- Left hemisphere – important for verbal information.
- Right hemisphere – retention of visual information.

Language

- Broca's area – at third frontal convolution of the left hemisphere; damage impairs language expression, but allows language comprehension.
- Wernicke's area – posteriorly in superior portions of temporal lobe; damage impairs language comprehension, but allows fluent speech.
- Language function is mainly controlled in the left hemisphere (although it may be in the right hemisphere for about 50% of left-handed individuals).
- However, non-language aspects of speech (e.g. pitch, flow, intonation) may be controlled by the right hemisphere.

Visuo-spatial ability

- Primary visual cortex resides in the occipital lobe.
- There are many 'maps' of the visual field in the primary visual cortex.
- Required, perhaps for different functions (e.g. colour, distances, movements, etc.).

Object recognition

- Visual object agnosia - isolated inability to recognise everyday objects (i.e. not due to deterioration in intellectual ability).
- Apperceptive agnosia – inability to collect the different information about the objects together to gain a full mental representation of the object.
- Associative agnosia – ability to form a mental picture of the object (e.g. able to draw it) without being able to recognise it.
- Prosopagnosia – difficulty in recognising people visually.
- Visual disorientation – the inability to reach out to pick objects due to lack of judgement about the relative positions of objects.

- Parietal lobe lesions may lead to visual agnostic deficits:
  - probably two major streams in the brain:- ventral (carrying information on 'what') and dorsal (carrying information on 'where').

Frontal lobe functions

Frontal lobe: premotor and motor cortex; prefrontal cortex.

- Premotor cortex – executive control area for the motor cortex.
- Prefrontal cortex:
  - Essential for planning of actions.
  - Damage: inability to make rational assessment of situations and make appropriate decisions; tendency towards preservation, inappropriate social behaviour. Patients may have difficulties with Wisconsin card-sorting test or Thurstone word fluency test:

  Wisconsin card-sorting test (a pack of cards which can be sorted in different ways; e.g. colour, shapes, number of shapes) – subjects have to sort out cards according to a pre-determined rule, which can be changed by the examiner.

  Thurlstone word fluency test – saying as many words as possible with a given letter.

- Norman and Shallice (prefrontal cortex in regulating behaviour) contention scheduling – the 'automatic pilot';

  supervisory activating system (SAS) – override automatic pilot, important in unfamiliar situations;

  SAS is impaired in patients with frontal lobe damage.

Psychological assessment

Principles of measurement

Scaling

- 4 levels of linear scales. In terms of sophistication:

  Categorical (nominal) scale – measurement based on classification (names) only (e.g. gender, different ethnic groups). The categories are not arranged in any order.

  Ordinal scale – the measures are ranked (e.g. social classes I–V). However, the differences between two categories are not the same (e.g. difference between social classes I and II is not the same as that between social classes II and III).

Interval scale – the measures are ranked and the differences between different scale points are meaningful (i.e. difference between a score of 10 and 20 is the same as a difference between a score of 20 and 30). However, the zero point is not meaningful (e.g. °C for temperature). Most psychological scales devised are of interval scales.

Ratio scale – the differences between different scale points are meaningful. Furthermore, the zero point is meaningful so that the ratio of a measurement to another is meaningful (i.e. a score of 20 is twice that of a score of 10).

- A linear scale usually measures only one dimension.
- Rating scales – may measure
  - levels of agreement with a certain statement (e.g. strongly agree–strongly disagree) as in Likert scale. The statement may represent positive or negative ends of the variable in question;
  - the variable in question (e.g. very happy–very sad).
- Reliability
  Inter-rater reliability – the level of agreement between different raters.
  Intra-rater reliability – the level of agreement of a single rater on different occasions.

Approaches to interpreting scores

Norm-referenced approach – comparison of raw scores with those obtained by a particular population. Hence, it involves comparison with the norm tables for different populations. Most psychological tests on personality and intelligence use this approach.

Criterion-referenced approach – the score is interpreted according to what the subject can actually do. It refers to the actual performance rather than comparison with other people.

Intelligence

Definition
Possible definitions include the ability to

- understand and use knowledge,
- learn from experience and apply it in new situations,
- reflect and be self-critical (metacognition),

(or a combination of these).

Components

- Studied by factor analysis. Factors uncovered include spatial, numerical, logical and verbal abilities.
- Spearman (1927): a single general factor (g) and other specific factors.
- Thurstone (1938): 7 independent factors:
  - numerical ability,
  - word fluency,
  - visualisation,
  - memory,
  - perceptual speed,
  - induction (discovering general rules from particular cases),
  - verbal reasoning (e.g. interpreting proverbs).
- Cattell (1971)
  fluid ability – e.g. the ability to manipulate information quickly.
  crystallised ability – acquired knowledge (e.g. general facts, vocabularies, etc.).
- Gardner (1983) – 7 separate types of intelligence with independent biological roots in the biological structure of the brain:
  - intellectual abilities (e.g. numerical skills),
  - physical abilities,
  - social abilities.

Intelligence quotient (IQ)

- Stern –

$$IQ = \left(\frac{\text{mental age}}{\text{chronological age}} \right) \times 100\%$$

i.e. comparing the average age of subjects in the population who would have achieved the same level of intelligence with the actual age of the subject; not appropriate in adulthood.
- Binet (basis of Stanford–Binet Intelligence Test) – Change to norm-referenced approach, comparing with the 'norm' within the population. The distribution of 'intelligence' in the population approximates the normal distribution. Assume mean = 100, standard deviation = 15.

Stability of intelligence quotient

- Stern's approach – IQ appears to decrease with age (in fact, it is inapplicable in adulthood).
- Binet's approach – probably fairly stable over time. Stability over time reflects the balance of genetic and environmental factors and their interaction.

Measurement of intelligence using specific tests
Wechsler scales – similar in principle to the Stanford–Binet Intelligence Scales:
- A series of tests of different abilities.
- Measure verbal, numerical and spatial reasoning and various types of short-term memory.
- Verbal and performances skills sections – separate tests of comprehension, information and reasoning.
- A graded series of similar tasks. Subscores depend on the most difficult question in a skill section a subject can answer.
- Gives a breakdown of the scores in different components (e.g. verbal, performance).

Cultural influences

- Intelligence tests may favour one population of subjects over others; e.g. different ethnic groups, rural and city dwellers, different languages.
- Caution is needed in interpreting intelligence test results.

Some basic neuropsychological tests

Flexible vs. pre-packaged batteries of test

- Flexible – examiner chooses a combination of tests specific for the patients.
- Pre-packaged – comprehensively test patients in all areas.

Welschler Adult Intelligence Scale

- 13 separate subtests – information, digit span, vocabulary, arithmetic, comprehension, similarities, picture completion, picture arrangement, block design, object assembly, digit symbol, symbol search, mazes.

Memory tests

- Wechsler Memory Scale – 18 separate sub-tests.
- Verbal memory tests: words, nonsense syllables, sentences, digits, Randt Memory Test, non-verbal memory tests (use geometric figures) – Benton Test of Visual Retention; Memory for Designs Test.

Cognitive functioning

- Abstract thinking.
  - verbal: proverb interpretation.
  - non-verbal: object sorting test, Winconsin Card Sorting Test, Halstead Category Test.

Verbal functioning tests

- Controlled Word Association Test, e.g. 'say as many words as possible beginning with ph'.
- Reitan–Indiana Aphasic Screening Test – includes items in naming, verbal, writing.

Attention, mental speed, etc

- Stroop Test, Continuous Performance Test.

Personality tests

- MMPI (Minnesota Multiphasic Personality Inventory) – personality and emotional status.
- 16-PF questionnaire.
- Projective tests: Thematic Apperception Test, Rorschach Inkblot Technique.

2 | Human development

Basic frameworks for conceptualising development

Nature and nurture

- Human development is a dynamic process.
- Both nature and nurture *interact* to influence development.
- The relative contribution of nature and nurture vary according to the trait in question. For example,
  - childhood motor developmental milestones are largely genetically determined;
  - social development is considerably influenced by environment.
- Example of interaction:
  - children require both intellectual potential and environmental stimuli for intellectual development;
  - children who are genetically more able are more likely to exploit environmental opportunities for learning.

Stage theories

- Development is an active, dynamic process influenced by both innate drives and social experiences.
- Development is regarded as an ordered sequence of hierarchical and discrete stages:
  - everyone follows the same stages;
  - each stage is different and becomes more complex as one progresses along the stages.
- Examples: Freudian theories (oral, anal, phallic stages); Piaget's theory of cognitive development; social learning model.
- Contrast with learning theories which see development as a continuous process.

Maturational tasks

- *Maturation* – genetic factors responsible for development.
- *Maturational* tasks – generally those which are determined largely by genetic factors (e.g. the age when a child sits up, walks, talks, etc.).
- Although environment plays a part, its role is restricted by biological limitations.
- For these tasks, it is not possible to enable a child to achieve a milestone before it is genetically ready.

Possible definitions of maturity

- A state of adulthood, completed growth or full functioning.
- The outcome of the process of biological unfolding.

Different types of maturity: sexual, emotional, physical, etc. Some types (e.g. emotional) require more subjective judgement than others (e.g. physical).

Methodology for studying development

Cross-sectional studies

- Data are gathered from a population at one point in time.
- Variables of interest (e.g. intelligence quotient, developmental milestones) of subjects are compared across different age groups.
- Alternatively, development (e.g. intelligence scores) is correlated with exposure to various environmental influences (e.g. different styles of teaching).
- *Advantages*:
  - cheap and quick to perform;
  - no need for follow-up.
- *Disadvantages*:
  - impossible to control for *cohort* effects (i.e. a group of people born at different times may have experienced different environmental factors);
  - individual variations may be large and hide any real effects.

Cohort studies

- A well-defined population of people is identified.
- The relevant variables of development and environmental factors are collected at regular intervals.

- *Advantages*:
  - no problems with cohort effect;
  - development of the same group of people are compared over time; hence, individual variations matter little.
- *Disadvantages*:
  - takes a long time to complete;
  - expensive to conduct;
  - subjects may drop out of study.

Individual studies

- Study of the development of individuals over a period of time; e.g., study of how children at different ages solve problems.
- May incorporate qualitative methods to explore the individual's perceptions and feelings (e.g. narrative or ethnographic research).
- Allows in-depth study of a few individuals.
- Difficult to generalise results across the population.

Identification and evaluation of influences

Cross-sectional study

Caution required due to possible (i) cohort effects and (ii) confounding variables.

Cohort study

- Need to ensure that results are based on comparison of scores over time at individual rather than at group level.
- Percentage changes are more important than absolute changes.
- Problems of 'regression to the mean'.
- Ensure dropouts have characteristics similar to subjects who completed the study.
- Association does not necessarily imply causation. Some factors which suggest causation include:
  - strength of the association (i.e. large effects);
  - dose–response relationship;
  - effects occurring after the possible influences,
  - plausible psychological or physiological explanations.

Attachment and bonding

Bowlby's attachment theory

Attachment – an intense, lasting emotional bond formed between infants and adults so that the infants will:

- approach them when distressed;
- show no fear of them at a time when they show fear of strangers;
- readily accept the care given by them;
- exhibit gross anxiety if separated from them.

Attachment process:

- pre-attachment, up to 3 months;
- indiscriminate attachment, 3–7 months;
- discriminate attachment, 7–9 months.

Bowlby's attachment theory:

- Attachment is controlled by genetic programming of both babies and mothers.
- Babies are innately programmed to shape their caregivers' behaviour specific to the species to maximise survival.
- Caregivers (usually mothers) are also programmed to respond to the babies.
- Bowlby believed that there is a critical period for attachment development, but this was found to be untrue.
- Bowlby believed that although multiple attachments can occur, attachment to the mother is unique, the first to appear, and the strongest. However, subsequent studies found that the father–child bond can be qualitatively similar to maternal bonding.

Types of attachment (partly adapted from Ainsworth et al., 1978 and Main, 1991)

Type	Name	Characteristics of baby
A	Anxious–avoidant	Indifferent to mother Shows no emotion when mother leaves or returns Easily comforted by strangers

B	Secure	Happy when mother is around
		Distressed when mother leaves
		When mother returns, seeks immediate contact and is comforted
		Stranger is only partially successful in comforting baby
C	Anxious–resistant	Ambivalent towards mother
		Difficult to settle when mother is present
		Distressed when mother leaves
		Ambivalent when mother returns
		Resistant to strangers' attempt to comfort
D	Insecure–disorganised	Acts as if mother is fear-inducing
		Attempts to seek proximity to mother also induces fear
		Incompatible goals of seeking and avoiding proximity

The prevalence of different types depend on culture.
Type B (secure attachment) is universally the commonest type (about three quarters of all attachments).

Conditions for secure attachment

- Mother's sensitivity (i.e. how she responds to baby's needs) is paramount.
- Characteristics of sensitive mothers:
  - perceive events from the baby's perspectives;
  - interpret baby's signal correctly;
  - respond to baby's needs promptly.

Clinical relevance of security of attachment

Secure attachment (type B) – Child more likely to

- be more curious,
- achieve higher social confidence,
- be independent at age 5,
- be free of behavioural problems.

Anxious–avoidant (type A) – Child more likely to

- have experienced long periods of separation from the attachment figure,
- be unsociable and non-independent later on,

- have reduced ability to empathise with others,
- have higher chance of neurotic symptoms in later childhood.

Anxious–resistant type (type C) – Child likely to

- be associated with child abuse or mistreatment,
- experience emotional problems later in childhood.

Early separation and its consequences

Short-term separation

- *Bowlby's 'maternal deprivation theory'* – broken mother–infant attachment in the first few years of life inevitably leads to serious developmental harm. Subsequent studies do not confirm this theory.
- Typical child's distress response to short-term separation: protest, despair, detachment.
- Factors modifying the child's response to separation: age, gender, previous relationship with attachment figure and previous separation.
- Multiple attachments (e.g. with child minders) can reduce distress.

Long-term separation (e.g. parental death)

- Severe separation anxiety possibly leading to school phobia and refusal in later childhood.
- Children of divorced parents have lower self-esteem, academic achievement, and more difficulties with psychological adjustment.
- Children who have experienced parental death are more likely to suffer from anxiety and depression in later life.
- Consequences of early parental death: grossly retarded language development, lack of attachment behaviour and social withdrawal.

Parental divorce

- Children whose parents divorce are more likely to experience emotional difficulties.
- Boys experience more problems than girls.
- Problems may occur before divorce due to inter-parental conflicts.
- Emotional problems are minimised by
  - minimising parental conflict;
  - consistent treatment of children by both parents;
  - accessibility of both parents after divorce.

Neonatal maternal bonding

Klaus and Kennell (1976) – *'extended contact hypothesis'*: 'Prolonged contact between mother and neonates leads to better attachment'. This influenced the hospital policy of not separating neonates and mother immediately after delivery.

However, such prolonged contact is not absolutely essential for good bonding:

- Successful bonding may occur many months after birth.
- Father–child bonding can be as strong as mother–child bonding.

Family relationship and parenting practice

Influence of parental attitudes and practice

Two important dimensions: emotional responsiveness and level of control.

Emotional responsiveness

- Children with 'warm' parents have fewer behavioural problems.
- Children with 'warm' parents are more likely to accept their values.

Level of control. 3 child-rearing styles (Baumrind):

Parental style	Characteristics	Consequences
Permissive	Laissez-Faire approach	Low social competencies
	Few demands on children	Low cognitive competencies, especially for boys
	Reluctant to punish inappropriate behaviour	Children may tend to be hostile and aggressive
Authoritative	Definite rules children are expected to follow	High social and cognitive competencies
	Rules derived after discussion with children	Enable children to develop internal standards
	Children's views are valued	Good interpersonal skills
	Generally use of rewards to enforce standards	

Authoritarian	Strict and enforced rules	Average social competencies
	Autocratic parents, little room for discussion	Generally low cognitive competencies
	Punishment used to secure compliance	

Distorted family functions

Parental discord and divorce
- Long term depression and social maladjustment may result.
- Difficult to disentangle the relative contributions of discord and divorce.

Overprotection – Overprotected children tend to
- seek the companionship of adults protecting them;
- avoid other children and peers for fear of rejection.

Rejection – Rejected children tend to
- be sad,
- be socially isolated,
- have low self-esteem,
- display undesirable social behaviours (e.g. aggression, lack of co-operation with peers).

Enmeshment
- Lack of a well-defined parent–child boundary.
- Difficult for children to develop internal standards.

Bereavement in early childhood

- Difficulty in establishing attachment behaviour.
- Difficulty in establishing positive relationship with others.
- Increased likelihood of anxiety and depression in adulthood.

Effects are partially reversible by alternative attachment figures (e.g. adoption).

Effects of intrafamilial abuse

- Associated with anxious–resistant attachment behaviour.
- Inappropriate social behaviour during childhood (e.g. aggression, inappropriate sexual behaviour).
- Profound adverse psychological effects in later childhood and adulthood, including:

- higher incidence of anxiety and depression,
- very poor self-esteem,
- difficulty in establishing a trusting relationship with others.

Non-orthodox family structure

- *Single parent family*:
  - associated with a higher incidence of child abuse;
  - may suffer from lack of stimulation due to relative lack of social support.
- *Family with homosexual couples*:
  - much social stigma attached;
  - however, no major adverse effects on child development found so far.

Temperament

Definition

Aspects of an individual's general make-up which govern his/her disposition towards a particular pattern of *emotional reactions, mood*, and *level of sensitivity*.

Typologies of individual temperamental differences

- Different babies have different temperaments.
- *Thomas and Chess (1977)* – 3 types of babies and children:
  Easy child – easygoing, predictable, sociable, perceived as adaptable.
  Difficult child – cries a lot, highly active, socially inhibited, unpredictable, perceived as unadaptable.
  Slow-to-warm-up child – between the difficult and the easy child.
- Over two-thirds are of the 'easy children' type.
- Significantly positive, but weak, correlation between temperament and subsequent school problems.
- No significant relationship found between temperament and later childhood personality.

Childhood vulnerability and resilience

- There are considerable variations amongst individuals regarding susceptibility to mental illness caused by adverse life events.

- In children, parental discord, physical and sexual abuse, early loss of attachment figures are significant stress factors which may predispose them to mental illness.
- The relationship between childhood exposure to these stressors and future vulnerability is complex and differs amongst individuals.

Cognitive development

- The thinking process and how it changes over time.

Piaget's model

- *Genetic epistemology* is the organisation of intelligence and how it changes as children grow.
- Cognitive development is an *active* process involving the interaction between innate ability and environmental events.
- Children achieve their development through their own actions (constructivist theory).
- Achieving cognitive equilibrium:
  - Children use psychological structures 'schema' as basic building blocks.
  - *Adaptation*: New information may be *assimilated* into existing schema, or *accommodated* (modified) to cope with new experiences.
  - A state of *cognitive equilibrium* is said to be achieved if a child can cope with all new experiences.

Piaget's stage theory

Cognitive development occurs through a series of fixed, pre-determined and universal *hierarchical* stages.
Each stage builds on earlier stages.
There are 4 stages of cognitive development:
1. *Sensorimotor stage* (< *2 years*)
   - Perception of the world through sensory information and action.
   - Gradual development of *object permanence* at about 1 year (knowing the existence of objects which are out of sight).
   - Improvement in problem-solving abilities by the development of memory, language and symbolic thought.

2. *Pre-operational stage (2–7 years)*
- Inability to execute operations (i.e. logical mental sequences of actions).
- *Egocentrism* (inability to view from the perspective of others); e.g. 'three mountains task'.
- *Seriation* task difficulties (arranging objects on a particular dimension) and *artificialism* (belief that nature has been constructed by people).
- *Transductive reasoning* (inferring relationship between two objects based on a single shared attribute; e.g., both birds and insects fly, hence birds are insects).
- *Animism* (belief that inanimate objects are alive).
- *Centration* – (focusing on a single quality at a time).
- *Inability of understanding conservation* (i.e. understanding that any quantity remains the same even if the physical arrangement is altered).

3. *Concrete operational stage (7–11 years)*
- Loss of egocentrism.
- Ability to
  - conserve and understand reversibility;
  - understand that an object can belong to more than one class (i.e. decentre);
  - solve transitivity tasks (e.g. A is bigger than B, and B is bigger than C. Which is bigger, A or C?) but only by arranging concrete physical objects, not by reasoning.

4. *Formal operational stage (11–adulthood)*
- Hypothetico-deductive reasoning – able to formulate and test hypotheses.
- Able to think hypothetically (i.e. the logical consequences of a false scenario).

Criticism of Piaget's model

Susequent experiments by Donaldson found that children could perform some tasks which Piaget considered them incapable of. These discrepancies may be because:

- the children may not have understood what was expected of them in Piaget's experiments;
- some of Piaget's experiments do not make 'human sense';

- in conservation tasks, children may be distracted by how the transformation occurs;
- Piaget did not take into account the social context.

The relevance of Piaget's model to communication with children

- Opportunities for active exploration and investigations are essential for children's development.
- Developing children's thinking is more important than achieving the final outcomes which adults perceive to be correct.
- The tasks must be appropriate for the children's stages of development – the children must be *ready*.
- Children's understanding of the explanation for various phenomena (e.g. death) depends on their stages of development.

Outline of language development in childhood

Sequence of language development

Almost universal amongst all cultures:

Pre-linguistic stage (before 1 year)
- Babbling at 6–9 months.
- Ends with development of *holophrase* (one-word phrase supplemented by gesture) at 1 year.

Two-word phrase (18 months to 3 years)
- Established vocabularies increase quickly to about 300 words at 2 years.
- Two-word phrase is essentially telegraphic, using words which convey the most information.
- Corresponds to acquisition of combination rules.

Complex grammar (3 years onwards)
- Vocabulary of about 1000 words established by 3 years.
- Mean length of utterance increased by including words missed out in previous telegraphic speech.
- Complex sentences acquired by 5 years.

- Application of grammar rules to language resulting in over-generalised language (e.g. mistaking the past participle 'done' for 'do-ed').
- Acquisition of a vocabulary of about 20,000 by 13 years.

Theories of language development

Piaget's view

- Language follows from children building their own schemata through active exploration of their environment.
- Grammar development reflects underlying general cognitive development.
- Logical thought follows from acquisition of operations, and language is an important tool for operational and symbolic thinking.
- Language merely reflects and is not the cause of cognitive development.

Skinner's view

- Language is acquired by operant conditioning, imitation of adults and shaping of responses.
- Grammar development is acquired by differential reinforcement.

Chomsky's view

- Children are innately equipped with a *language acquisition device* (LAD) which consists of *transformational grammar* (TG).
- Children use LAD to look for *linguistic universals* (e.g. consonants, vowels and syllables). This explains why children can:
  - easily learn any language they are exposed to,
  - acquire grammatical rules even when exposed to ungrammatical speech.
- 2 levels of structure: *Surface* – actual speech, unique to specific languages; *Deep* – the meaning of speech, applies universally.

Vygotsky's view

- Language arises from internalisation of social relationships.
- The acquisition of language comes before the development of thought.

Interactive model

- Inborn ability and environment influences interact to develop language.

Social competence and relationships with peers

Development of social competence

Infancy – development of secure attachment important.

Older babies – make regular social contacts with one another e.g. gazing, touching, offering play materials (Goldschmied).

Toddlers – play together; e.g., reciprocal imitation for young toddlers.

Later – complex interactions between social experience, personality, and environment.

Children without siblings – variety of development amongst these children, but generally have as much chance of positive emotional and social development as children with siblings (Laybourn).

Theories

Behaviourism – social competence achieved through reinforcement and shaping.

Social learning theory (Bandura) – learning by modelling and observation.

Ethology – innate tendency to form social relationships (e.g. bonding with mother).

Social cognition approaches (arises from Piaget's work)

- Empathy requires understanding of other's points of view and responding appropriately.
- Children in the pre-operational stage are egocentric. (This assertion is strongly contested.)
- Social thinking is developed in stages (e.g. from surface, simple, rigid, egocentric and diffuse to deep, complex, flexible, altruistic and organised).

Group formation and acceptance

Age 3: Social mixing (usually children of same sex) increases. Play usually solitary (on their own) or parallel (alongside other children).

Ages 4–6: More complex play.

Ages 6–8: Start of group formation.

Age 8 onwards: Complex and formal groups.

Features of group:

- interact regularly,
- share norms determining how members behave,

- foster a sense of belonging,
- have a structure for the group to work towards certain goals.

Friendships

- Reciprocal relationships between peers.
- Up to a fifth of all children below 5 have imaginary friends.
- Criteria for choice of friendship changes with age (Bigelow):
  Reward-cost stage (7–8 years) – living nearby with interesting toys and enjoying similar games.
  Normative stage (10–11 years) – common values, beliefs, loyalty and co-operation.
  Empathic stage (10–12 years) – common interests, ability to understand one another, share personal information, and respond sensitively to one's disclosure.
  Above 12 years – emotional exchanges become important.

Isolation and rejection

- Possible causes: immaturity, lack of intelligence, lack of physical attractiveness and peer sensitivity.
- Are significant predictors of future maladjustment and offending behaviour.
- Tend to be stable over childhood and adolescence.
- Rejected children tend to be miserable and have low self-esteem.

The components of popularity

- Personality traits and sensitivity to peers are important.
- Children with mesomorphic (athletic build) features preferred (Staffieri).
- *Boys* – early maturers more confident and popular (Clausen).
- *Girls* – early maturers do not have advantages over later maturers.
- Perceived facial attractiveness and sensitive authoritative parenting important.

Moral development

Freud's theory

- Morality is determined by the *superego*.
- Oedipus complex is resolved by identifying with the same-sex parent.

That parent's image is introjected into the child's ego to form the superego.
- For boys, fear of castration is the prime motive for identifying with the father.
- However, contrary to the theory, boys are not more moral than girls.

Piaget's theory

- Humans have no moral basis at birth.
- Heteronomous stage (rigid moral reasoning) (ages 5–11):
  – moral rules are perceived as unchangeable and handed down by authorities (e.g. parents or God);
  – morality is judged more by the *consequences* of the actions than by original motives.
- Autonomous stage (moral co-operation) (aged above 11):
  – coincides with formal operational thinking in cognitive development;
  – morality is judged by the motives of the person involved.

> ### Critique

  – Focus on theoretical morality than on practical morality.
  – Younger children may be less able to distinguish and express differences between motives and consequences.

Kohlberg's stage theory

The theory is based on the observations of children's responses to the moral dilemma of Heinz whose wife will die unless an expensive drug (which Heinz cannot afford to buy) is available.

Level 1 – pre-conventional morality

Stage 1 (punishment and obedience orientation) – What is punishable or not determines entirely whether an action is right or wrong.

Stage 2 (instrumental orientation) – Whether an action brings rewards or harm determines entirely whether an action is right or wrong.

Level 2 – Conventional morality

Stage 3 (good interpersonal relationship orientation, 'good boy, nice girl') – Being a good person in the eyes of others renders an action right.

Stage 4 (social order orientation) – An action which 'maintains a good social order and respects authorities' is right.

Level 3 – Post-conventional morality

Stage 5 (social contract–legalistic orientation) – Laws established by democracy should be respected. However, extreme circumstances (e.g. life-saving) may justify laws being broken.

Stage 6 (universal ethical principles orientation) – A person's own conscience operating according to certain universal principles determines whether an action is right or wrong.

Critique

– Methodology biased towards Western cultures and educated people.
– Kohlberg's study based on *male's* definition of morality.
– Concerned with moral thinking rather than moral behaviour.
– Kohlberg's subjects lived through certain social changes (civil rights movements) and the results may not be generalisable.

Selman's stages of social perspective development

- Stage 0 (3–6 years). Egocentric thinking – are unable to distinguish between the views of themselves and others.
- Stage 1 (6–8 years). Social informational role taking – understand that others may have a different perspective, but might not know that others realise this as well.
- Stage 2 (8–10 years). Self-reflection – understand that others may have a different perspective, and that others realise this as well.
- Stage 3 (10–12 years). Mutual role taking – understand people from a neutral bystander's perspective.
- Stage 4 (over 12 years). Social and conventional system role taking – understand that beliefs may be determined and operate within a system of shared perspectives (e.g. cultural and religious views).

Fears in childhood and adolescence

Fears – a complex pattern of subjective, physiological and motor reactions to a real or imagined threat.

Young children

- *Stranger anxiety*
  - usually develops between 8 months and 1 year;
  - probably arises from (a) the infant's ability to compare the pattern of a known person's face with that of a stranger, and (b) object permanence;
  - rarely persists into 'social anxiety disorder' in adolescence.
- *Separation anxiety*
  - usually appears at about 8 months and disappears by about 18 months;
  - aetiology similar to stranger anxiety;
  - rarely becomes a disorder unless fears persist to become unrealistic and excessive after the age of 3.

Older children (>5 years)

Fears of
- Animals,
- Darkness,
- Separation.

Adolescents

Fears of
- Examinations,
- Physical health,
- Animals.

Sexual development

Definitions

Sex – biological make-up as 'male' or 'female'.
Gender – how we classify ourselves and others as 'men' or 'women'.
Ways of classifying biological sex
- chromosomal sex (e.g. XX or XY);
- gonadal sex (i.e. presence of testis or ovaries);

- sex of reproductive structures (e.g. uterus, fallopian tubes, epididymis);
- sex of external genitalia (e.g. penis, scrotum, clitoris).
  Note: Although these 4 ways of classification usually yield the same results, they can, in rare cases, differ (e.g. testicular feminisation syndrome has male chromosomal sex but female external genitalia).

Ways of classifying sex by non-biological factors
- sexual assignment at birth;
- sex of rearing;
- sex-role adoption (i.e. internalisation of characteristics appropriate for one sex or the other);
- gender-role identity (i.e. one's view of whether one is a man or a woman).

Sexual preference – whether one prefers a man or a woman as a sexual partner.

Development of gender and sex-role identity

Biosocial theory

- Interaction between biological and social factors.
- Others' reaction to a person's perceived biological sex becomes part of his or her social environment.
- Gender roles are *learned* (e.g. a boy whose penis was accidentally cut off during circumcision was successfully reared as female).

Psychoanalytic Theory   Gender identity is acquired through identification with the same-sex parent, which also resolves the Oedipus complex.

Social learning Theory   Boys and girls are treated differently by others (especially parents). Sex-appropriate behaviours are selectively reinforced.

Cognitive Developmental Theory   There are 3 stages:

1) *Gender labelling (3 years)* – Child discovers his/her own sex, but does not yet realise that it will invariably remain the same sex as an adult.
2) *Gender stability (4–5 years)* – Child recognises that people retain their gender throughout their life, but still depends on superficial

signs (e.g. length of hair or presence of beard) to determine their gender.

3) *Gender constancy or consistency (6–7 years)* – Child realises that gender is unchangeable (i.e. a woman remains so even when her hair is cut very short), similar to 'conservation' in Piaget's experiments.

Adolescence

Definition

- 'Grow into maturity'.
- May span from ages 11 to 20, beginning at puberty.
- Considerable changes in physiology, expectations, psychology.

Puberty

- Signals the onset of adolescence.
- Physical, psychological and hormonal changes.
- Girls have earlier puberty than boys by about 2 years.
- Gradual trend towards earlier puberty in the last century.
- Physical changes
  - uniform universal sequence, but age of onset and rate of development differ amongst individuals;
  - growth spurt and secondary sexual characteristics.
- Secondary sexual characteristics
  Boys – voice deepening, testes and penis enlarging, pubic and facial hair, first ejaculation.
  Girls – breast enlargement, axillary and pubic hair, menstruation.
- Earlier puberty in boys associated with increased popularity, but not in girls.

Classical views of adolescence

- 'Storm and stress',
- Identity crisis,
- Generation gap (although this may be disputed).

Common problems during adolescence

- Conflicts with parents,
- Fear of rejection by peers,
- Anxiety over relationship with members of the other sex.

Theories of adolescence

Hall's theory

- A person's development recapitulates the biological and cultural evolution of humans.
- Adolescence is a time of 'storm and stress' reflecting the history of the human race over the last several thousand years.
- Emotional reactions in adolescents are more intense.

Critique

No evidence to suggest that adolescents are more stressed than children or adults.

Erickson's epigenetic principle

- Fixed, genetically pre-determined processes of social and psychological development.
- Conflicts encountered in 8 psychosocial stages of psychosocial development:

Infancy	Trust vs mistrust
2–3 years	Autonomy vs shame and doubt
3–5 years	Initiative vs guilt
6–11 years	Industry vs inferiority
Adolescence	Identity vs role confusion
Early adulthood	Intimacy vs isolation
Middle age	Generativity vs stagnation
Old age	Integrity vs despair

- Adolescents must establish a strong sense of personal *identity* to find a place in adult society. The identity and role confusion may create problems.
- However, Western cultures often view adolescence as a *moratorium* (i.e. sanctioned delay of adulthood), which makes transition difficult.
- Adult identity depends largely on an occupational role. Drifting through a series of social and occupation roles results in role confusion.

Marcia's 4 identity formation

Maladaptive

- *Identity formation* – in crisis, no self-definition or goals.
- *Identity foreclosure* – rash and hasty commitment to certain conventional goals.

Healthy

- *Identity moratorium* – postponement of identity and experimentation with different alternatives.
- *Identity achievement* – achievement of definite goals and commitments after going through crisis.

Early adult life

Common adaptations

- Courting and getting married.
- Starting a new family with children.
- Pursuing a career.

Factors affecting how well one adapts psychologically

- Age and choice of life plan.
- Social expectations (e.g. expectations of marriage and having children were stronger in the past).
- Enormous individual variations.

Courting and marriage

- Married people in general
  - are healthier,
  - live longer,
  - suffer less mental illness.
- Men benefit more from marriage than women in terms of emotional support.
- Marriage: financial, family and personal responsibility.
- High incidence of mental distress at the time of deciding to get married.

Being parents

- Has different meanings for different individuals (e.g. meeting demands of partners, as fulfilling a drive towards 'generativity', etc.).

- Expectations of having children less with modern contraception and the feminist movement.
- *Advantages*: sense of fulfilment and being needed; enhanced self-esteem.
- *Disadvantages*: risks of men feeling neglected when children are born; financial strain; childcare problems for women.

Personal identity in adult life

Erickson's psychosocial stages

- See Erickson's psychosocial stages above.
- *Early adulthood (before 40)*
  - Need for intimacy (formation of deep personal relationships) to achieve psychosocial status of adulthood; fear of isolation (failure to love others).
  - Strong identity needed before intimacy can be achieved.
- *Middle aged (40–60)*
  - Need for generativity (expansion of interests and caring for others). Otherwise, stagnation (turning inward toward one's own needs and comfort) results.

Critique

Psychosocial stages may differ between sexes and cultures. For example, women may be more likely to achieve intimacy with occupational identity.

Levinson et al.'s "Seasons of a Man's Life" (based on in-depth interviews with middle-aged men)

Life-structure theory – adult development consists of a sequence of 4 *eras* which overlap by about 5 years to form *cross-era transitions*:

Eras
1. Pre-adulthood (< 22).
2. Early adulthood (17–45).
3. Middle adulthood (40–65).
4. Late adulthood (> 60).

Cross-era transitions

1. Early adult transition (17–22):
   - struggling to form adult identity;
   - coping with separation (e.g. leaving home) and attachment (exploring the world).
2. Middle-life transition (40–45) – see 'Mid-life crisis' below.
3. Late adult transition (60–65):
   - getting old;
   - retirement.

Mid-life crisis

- Levinson considered it as inevitable and necessary.
- Possible features:
  - review achievement and ambitions, and accept that not all goals will be fulfilled;
  - make choices of a new life structure;
  - experience 'empty nest' syndrome;
  - realise the prospect of getting old and the possibility of death;
  - experience tension between separation and attachment;
  - respond by personal growth or by changing the external aspects of their lives (e.g. divorce, change occupations).

Critique

Subsequent studies found that a large proportion of middle-aged people feel more positive about life. Hence, it is not universal.

Identities

Common types of identity

- Work identity,
- Ethnic identity,
- Gender identity,
- Family role.

Work identity

- The type of job which one does.
- Contributes significantly to self-identity.
- Factors affecting how we select an occupation (Rybash et al.):

- fulfilment of self-concept;
- gradual shaping through fantasy, provisional and realistic considerations;
- match between personality and occupational demands.
• Typical processes of achieving work identity:
  - identifying a 'dream' occupation;
  - socialising into the occupation through career entry, training and mentoring;
  - adjusting discrepancy between expectation and reality;
  - either settling down for a stable career or changing direction until a suitable career is found.
• Significantly affected by local and national, and social and economic conditions.

Ethnic identity

Ethnic identity is easier achieved
• in a society with a dominant culture (if one belongs to the majority group);
• in a multicultural society than for minority members in a culture with a dominant culture;
• when the culture of one's origin and that of the dominant society is congruent;
• when the culture in the family and in society is congruent;
• in the absence of a negative stereotype of the culture one belongs to;
• in the absence of actual discrimination.

Gender identity and roles

• Gender roles begin in early childhood.
• In adulthood, gender role depends on societal stereotypes: e.g. *female –* empathetic, warm, tender feelings, bringing up children; *male –* aggressive, ambitious, provides for family.
• Gender roles develop as one internalises the societal stereotypes.
• Stages of development differ between male and female. (Men tend to achieve personal identity and independence before intimacy. The two may go hand in hand for women.)
• Adults who deviate from the societal expectation of their gender role tend to suffer more psychological distress.
• From middle age onwards, people tend to acquire more attributes and roles of the other sex (i.e. less polarised).

Normal ageing and its impact

Different types of 'ages'

Chronological age – the actual official age.
Biological age – the average age of people with the same state of facial appearance and body state.
Subjective age – how old people feel themselves to be.
Functional/social age – reflecting the lifestyle, family, work and the social role one plays.

Physical impact of ageing

Smaller – reduction in height, body mass, calcium store.
Slower – reduced reaction time, walking and working speeds.
Weaker – reduction in muscle strength and increased vulnerability to fractures.
Less elastic tissue – causing wrinkles, atherosclerosis, etc.
Fewer body parts – e.g. hair, teeth.
Reduced sensory functions – e.g. vision, hearing, etc.
Disease – higher incidence of most diseases, especially cardiovascular disease and cancers. Diseases may be chronic, which may give rise to impairment (anatomical defect), disability (functional limitation) and handicap (reduced functional capacity leading to loss of social function).

Cognitive impact of ageing

Intelligence

- Earlier cross-sectional studies appear to show that intelligence decreases with ageing. These results may be biased by cohort effect.
- However, later longitudinal studies (e.g. Seattle Longitudinal study) showed that intelligence was maintained until at least age 60.
- *Crystallised intelligence* – accumulated knowledge (e.g. reasoning and language skills); increases with age.
- *Fluid intelligence* – the ability to solve novel and unusual problems; decreases with age.

Memory

- Little or no decline in sensory and short–term memory with age.
- Large decline in selective attention (i.e. attempt to concentrate in the presence of distraction) and long–term memory.
- No decline in semantic memory (i.e. general facts and information) but slight decline in episodic memory.
- Negative stereotype (e.g. that older people are forgetful) may act as self-fulfilling prophecy.

Social impact of ageing

Risk of loss of daily routine and social isolation due to

- retirement,
- restriction in mobility due to illness,
- children leaving home,
- bereavement and loss of friends, relatives and spouse.

Social disengagement theory (Cumming and Henry, 1961)

- Disengagement *inevitable* due to unwritten contract between society and individuals.
- Mutual withdrawal of individual from society: society demands older people to be replaced by younger people; individuals choose to reduce social activities.
- Results in older people having reduced social contact, increased individuality, and withdrawal to prepare for changes and death.

Critique

The theory is not constructive to the well-being of older people; not every old person disengages (e.g. some undertake voluntary work).

Re-engagement theory of ageing

- Older people have the same psychosocial needs as middle-aged people.
- Decreased social activity is not mutual, but is due to society withdrawing from individuals.
- Optimal ageing involves staying active to resist social isolation.

Critique

Lack of empirical support.

Social exchange theory (Dyson, 1980)

- Contract between individuals and society.
- Exchange of economically active roles for increased leisure time and reduced responsibility when we retire.

Erickson's psychosocial theory

- Conflict between ego-integrity (satisfaction with the success and failures of life) and despair (feeling unfulfilled and fearing death).

Emotional impact of ageing

- Disengagement – actual emotional impact depends heavily on the personality of the individual.
- More reminiscences of their lives – the well-adjusted older people enjoy reminiscences more than the ill-adjusted ones.
- Tendency to become more introverted and more accommodative (acceptance of adverse circumstances) with age.

Disability and pain

Disability

- Differences between impairment, disability and pain:
  Impairment – physical or psychological defects (e.g. ischaemia to organs).
  Disability – inability to perform certain activities due to impairment (e.g. inability to walk).
  Handicap – social consequences as a result of the disability (e.g. inability to work, reduced social contact, etc.).
- Disease, chronic illness and disability are more common in old age.
- Psychological consequences of illness (Sidell, 1995):
  - loss of self,
  - disrupted family and personal biographies,
  - loss of meaning – 'Why me?',
  - uncertainty and unpredictability,
  - isolation.

- Effects on caregiver:
  - primary strain (need to provide care);
  - secondary role strain (consequences on other roles, e.g. work);
  - secondary intrapsychic strain (e.g. self-esteem).

Pain

- Patients with chronic pain are more likely to
  - be depressed,
  - have reduced social contact,
  - have low self-esteem.
- In many cases, chronic pain has a physical cause.
- In some cases, chronic pain has no physical cause, but may be explained by reinforcement.
- Chronic pain may be reinforced by:
  Primary gain – e.g. sympathy from others due to the pain.
  Secondary gain – e.g. improved housing or financial benefits due to pain.

Death and dying

Bereavement and loss – death of others

- 4 phases after bereavement (Parkes, 1972):
  Numbness – shocked and in disbelief.
  Yearning – longs for deceased to return.
  Disorganisation and despair – realises that deceased will not return; realisation may be accompanied by anger and guilt feelings.
  Reorganisation – able to reorganise life and develop close relationship with others.
- Individuals vary in the length of time spent in each stage.

Preparing for death

- Before death, people fear pain and loss of dependency and dignity.
- 5 phases after a diagnosis of terminal illness:
  - denial,
  - anger,
  - bargaining,
  - depression,
  - acceptance.

3 | Psychopathology

Descriptive psychopathology

Basic concepts

Psychopathology – systematic study of abnormal experience, cognition and behaviour.
Descriptive vs dynamic psychopathology

Descriptive psychopathology	Dynamic (analytic) psychopathology
Categorisation of patient's abnormal experiences subjectively described (e.g. as feelings or thoughts) or as observed (as behaviour)	Explores underlying roots of behaviour and experience
Emphasis on conscious state	Emphasis on unconscious conflicts as possible causes for conscious experience
Study by observing and interviewing patients with empathy	Therapist–patient relationship used as tool in exploring unconscious conflicts (e.g. by transference)
Emphasis on form for categorisation and diagnosis	Emphasis on content

Phenomenology – study of psychic events and psychological feelings as phenomena without exploring the underlying causes. Requires empathy to elicit.

Form and content
   Form – description of the structure of abnormal experiences as categorised by descriptive psychopathology (e.g. delusions, hallucinations).
   Content – the actual abnormal experience (e.g. the feeling that one is the victim of persecution).
Primary and secondary symptoms
   Primary symptoms – symptoms which cannot be reduced further by understanding.
   Secondary symptoms – symptoms which arise from primary symptoms (e.g. delusions arising from hallucinations).

Disturbed consciousness

Unconsciousness

3 possible meanings:

- as in coma caused by organic brain disease (used in descriptive psychopathology);
- as in deep sleep;
- as in repression of memories too painful to acknowledge (used in analytic psychopathology).

Dimensions of consciousness

Vigilance–drowsiness – the ability to stay alert deliberately when otherwise one might become drowsy or asleep.
Lucidity–clouding – the level of awareness of internal and external stimuli.
Consciousness of self – the ability to experience, and an awareness of self.

Abnormal quantitative changes in consciousness
(as defined in descriptive psychopathology)

Heightened consciousness – subjective sense of richer perception; exhilarated mood; synaesthesiae (stimulus to one sensory modality results in sensory experience in another). Caused by:
- special events (e.g. falling in love, religious conversion);
- drugs (e.g. LSD, amphetamines);
- psychosis (e.g. mania, schizophrenia).

Diminished consciousness – a quantitative spectrum from normal, clouding, drowsiness, sopor, coma to death; important in the assessment of acute organic state (e.g. due to brain injury, metabolic disorder, toxic state or drug overdose).

Clouding of consciousness – impairment of consciousness, slight drowsiness, difficulty in concentration and attention.

Drowsiness – tendency to drift into unconsciousness, but kept awake with constant stimuli; subjective sleepiness; slurred speech, slow actions; reduced muscle tone.

Sopor – mostly unconsciousness, but temporarily kept awake by strong stimuli.

Coma – unarousable even with strong stimuli.

Abnormal qualitative changes in consciousness

Delirium – According to ICD 10, the symptoms present in *each* one of the following areas for a total period of less than 6 months:
- Impairment of consciousness and attention.
- Global disturbance of cognition (e.g. illusions, hallucinations, perceptual distortions).
- Psychomotor disturbance – e.g. hypo- or hyperactivity, unpredictable changes from one to the other.
- Sleep disturbance – e.g. insomnia, worsening of symptoms at night, disturbing dreams or nightmares.
- Emotional disturbance – e.g. depression, anxiety, irritability.

Confusion – A term not clearly defined. Loosely refers to loss of capacity for clear and coherent thought.

Stupor
- Reduction in spontaneous speech (i.e. mutism) and activity (i.e. akinesis).
- Reduction in reactivity to the environment.
- Usually some degree of clouding of consciousness.
- May occur with schizophrenia, mania, depression, dissociation and tumour in the diencephalon.

Epileptic automatism

- A state of clouding of consciousness during or immediately after a seizure, during which posture and muscle tone are maintained.
- The individual may perform actions without being aware of what is happening.
- Commonly associated with temporal lobe epilepsy.

Disturbed attention, concentration and orientation

Attention, concentration and orientation are important tests of cognitive functions.

Attention

- Voluntary or involuntary focusing of consciousness on a task.
- May be reduced
  normally: sleep, hypnotic state, tiredness, boredom;
  abnormally: organic states (e.g. brain injury, drug or alcohol induced, metabolic disturbance, etc.), in mania or dissociation.
- May be *narrowed* in depression (by preoccupation with morbid themes).

Concentration

- The maintenance of voluntary or involuntary focusing of consciousness on the task.
- May be reduced in organic state, in mania (due to increased distractibility) or in psychosis (due to having to concentrate on listening to voices).

Orientation

- The awareness of one's setting in terms of time, place and person.
- Disorientation in time occurs earliest – ranges from inaccuracy by more than an hour for the time of day to incorrect day of the week, the month, or even the year.
- Disorientation in place occurs next, followed by failure to identify other persons.
- Failure to know one's own name occurs in the most advanced stage.

Disturbed memory

Functions of memory and their impairment:

Functions	Meaning	Impairment
Registration	Capacity to hold new material	E.g., Inability to understand perceptions in acute confusional state E.g., anterograde amnesia following head injury E.g., palimpest (alcoholic black-out)

Retention	Ability to store material which can be returned to consciousness	Retrograde amnesia after head injury After temporal lobectomy
Retrieval	Capacity to return stored material from memory	Korsakov syndrome
Recall	Return of stored material to consciousness at a chosen moment	Usually psychological E.g. anxiety (during MRCPsych examination); dissociative fugue
Recognition	Feeling of familiarity when stored material is returned to consciousness	Usually due to organic disorder E.g. Korsakov syndrome

Identifying paramnesia

Jamais vu – loss of feeling of familiarity with events which one had previously met.

Déjà vu – a feeling of familiarity with events which one had not previously met.

Occurs in normal subjects, and subjects with anxiety, and temporal lobe epilepsy.

Confabulation

- Memory falsification in clear consciousness in amnesia due to organic disorders.
- Typically seen in early stages of Korsakov syndrome.
- Subjects give elaborate details of events which did not occur.
- Marked suggestibility.
- Possible explanations:
  - attempt to hide embarrassment;
  - reflects normal recall mechanisms;
  - fantastic nature.

Other memory falsification

Affective disorder – selective forgetting and inaccuracy of recall (para-mnesia) may occur, being consistent with current mood state (i.e. depressed patients falsify pessimistic material).
Pseudologia fantastica – fluent untruthful statements. Associated with hysterical behaviour.
Schizophrenia – initially correctly remembered material taking on a new meaning (delusional retrospective falsification); different from delusional memory (i.e. delusional experience described as memory).

Perseveration

- Production of appropriate response to the first stimulus, but repetition of the same response for subsequent stimuli where it is inappropriate.
- Occurs with clouding of consciousness.
- Pathognomonic of organic brain disease.

Psychogenic memory disturbance

Cryptamnesia – failure to remember that one is remembering (e.g. believing that an argument is original when one has heard it from others before).
Dissociative memory – loss of memory of a traumatic nature not attributable to organic mental disorder, intoxication or ordinary forgetfulness.
Dissociative fugue
- features of dissociative memory;
- purposeful travel beyond the usual everyday range; but maintenance of basic self-care and social interactions with strangers.
Approximate answers – e.g. answering '5' when asked 'what is 2+2'. Associated with hysterical pseudodementia, some organic conditions, and Ganser syndrome (in which other dissociative symptoms and clouding of consciousness occur).
Multiple personality disorder – apparent existence of two or more distinct personalities (with different memories, behaviour and preferences) within an individual, with only one being evident at any one time.

Perception

3 stages of perception
Awareness of:

- stimulus (e.g. a sound or image),
- configuration (i.e. sensory percept),
- entity.

Sensory percept and imagery

Sensory percept – caused by real stimulus, perceived as real, acted upon. *Imagery* – a fantasy, created voluntarily, not perceived as real, usually not acted upon.

Abnormal perception

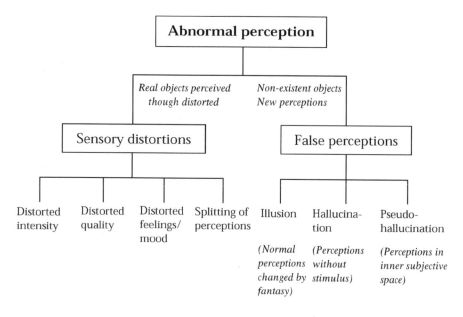

- Sensory distortions: real perceptual objects that are perceived to be distorted.
- False perceptions: non-existent objects; new perceptions which may or may not be in response to external simulus (e.g. illusions, hallucinations, pseudohallucinations).

Sensory distortions

Distorted intensity

Heightened perception: e.g. hyperacusis (normal sound seems deafening), visual hyperaesthesia (normal colours appear intense). Often occurs in mania.

Diminished perception: e.g. 'Everything appears dull.' Often occurs in depression.

Distorted quality: Often occurs in acute organic states and epilepsy. Examples are:

Macropsia – objects appear larger than their real size.

Micropsia – objects appear smaller than their real size.

Distorted feelings associated with perception

Derealization – feeling as if the world were unreal.

Depersonalisation – feeling as if the subject were unreal.

Ecstasy state – ordinary objects perceived as being extraordinary (e.g. in substance misuse).

Loss of intensity of feelings and enjoyment – e.g. in depression.

Splitting of perception: Inability to link two or more different modalities of perceptions from a single source. Often occurs in schizophrenia. For example, inability to link the facial expression and the speech of the person the individual is conversing with.

False perception

Illusions: They are natural perceptions transformed by the subject's fantasy. Often occur in normal subjects.

Completion illusion – e.g., a person desperate to visit the toilet may misinterpret 'to let' sign as 'toilet'.

Affect illusion – perception altered by mood state; e.g., a child waking up at night may momentarily interpret a wardrobe as a person.

Pareidolia illusion – images are perceived from shapes or patterns.

Whilst completion illusion and affect illusion disappear with attention, pareidolia illusion does not.

Hallucinations: They are perceptions in the absence of an external stimulus, and may occur in any of the five special senses. They have the following features:

• experienced as sensation and not as thought or fantasy;
• subject feels certain that the perception is real;
• cannot be altered by the subject – is involuntary;
• cannot be changed with reasoning by others.

Hallucinations usually represent an abnormal mental state. Different types of hallucinations will be discussed later.

Pseudohallucinations: These lie somewhere between fantasy and hallucination. They are perceptual experiences which

- occur in inner subjective space and not in external objective space;
- are not concrete or 'real';
- cannot be voluntarily evoked.

Pseudohallucinations often occur in widows or widowers who 'see' their dead spouse. They usually do not indicate an abnormal mental state.

Different types of hallucinations

Auditory hallucinations
- *Elementary hallucinations* – hearing unstructured sounds (e.g. noises).
- *Second person hallucinations* – may occur in organic states or schizophrenia.
- *Third person hallucinations*.
- *Running commentary* on subject's actions.
- *Audible thoughts* – characteristic of schizophrenia.

Visual hallucinations
- Characteristically occur in organic states. May occur together with auditory hallucinations.
- *Lilliputian hallucinations* – visual hallucinations of little animals or an army of small men. Often occur in delirium tremens following alcohol withdrawal.
- *Synaesthesiae* – a sensory stimulus in one modality perceived as from another modality (e.g. the subject 'sees' by the stimulus of sound, or 'hears' on visual stimulus).
- May occur in substance misuse (e.g. LSD).

Hallucinations of bodily sensation
- *Haptic or tactile hallucinations* – there is usually a delusional component; occurs in schizophrenia or drug withdrawal.
- *Formication* – feeling that insects are crawling over the body. May occur in drug (especially cocaine) or alcohol withdrawal.
- *Kinaesthetic hallucinations* – e.g. feeling that limbs are twisted: occur in schizophrenia.

Olfactory or gustatory hallucinations
- Hallucinations in smell or taste.
- May occur in schizophrenia, temporal lobe epilepsy and other organic states.

Extracampine hallucinations
- Hallucinations experienced outside the limits of sensory field (e.g. seeing a person in a different city).
- May occur in schizophrenia, temporal lobe epilepsy, or organic states.

Hypnagogic and hypnopompic hallucinations
- May be visual, auditory or tactile.
- *Hypnagogic hallucinations* – hallucinations whilst going to sleep.
- *Hypnopompic hallucinations* – hallucinations upon waking.
- Often occur in normal subjects.

Functional hallucinations
- Hallucinations which occur only with an unrelated external stimulus in the same modality.
- Both normal perception of the stimulus and the triggered hallucination are perceived at the same time; e.g., a patient with schizophrenia hearing running commentaries of his actions triggered by the sound of an engine. The patient hears both the engine and the running commentary simultaneously.

Reflex hallucinations
- Hallucinations in one sensory modality produced by stimulus in another modality; e.g., a patient with schizophrenia who feels pain on his limb whenever he sees a workman hammering.

Disorders in beliefs

Definition of delusions
Beliefs or ideas which are

- held with unusual conviction (unshakeable),
- illogical,
- clearly manifest as absurd or wrong to others (usually incongruent with the person's educational and cultural background).

Delusion describes the *form* of thought, not content.

Primary and secondary delusions

- *Primary*: Delusion not occurring in response to other psychopathological features (e.g. abnormal mood):
  - beliefs which are 'ultimately un-understandable';
  - pathognomonic of schizophrenia.

- *Secondary*: Delusion understandable from other psychopathological features:
  - e.g. delusions of a pessimistic nature in depression;
  - e.g. delusions of a grandiose nature in mania.

Delusional intuition, percept, atmosphere and memory

Delusional intuition (autochthonous delusion)
- delusions arising out of the blue in a single step;
- usually self-referent and of considerable significance to the patient.

Delusional percept
- a normal perception interpreted with delusional meaning;
- meaning usually referred to self; subjectively significant meaning, false (e.g. interpreting the changing of a red traffic light as meaning that one is the Queen of England);
- a first-rank symptom of schizophrenia;
- a type of primary delusion (*N.B.* Not all primary delusions are delusional percept).

Delusional atmosphere
- feeling that something sinister involving oneself is going on, though cannot be more definite;
- feeling of anticipation that events will soon fit together to form something significant (this feeling is called 'delusional mood');
- when delusion is formed, the subject is often relieved that the uncomfortable feeling is over;

N.B. Delusional atmosphere → mood → delusion.

Delusional memory
- 'retrospective delusion' – a subject believes (wrongly) that he/she remembers an event or idea which is clearly delusional to others;
- if delusional meaning is attached to such memory, it may result in delusional percept.

Factors in forming and maintaining delusions

Factors in formation (Brockington, 1991):
- brain functioning disorders,
- sensitive personality,
- need to maintain self-esteem,
- mood,
- reaction to perceptual disturbance,

- reaction to depersonalisation,
- cognitive overload.

Maintenance factors

- need for consistency;
- communication difficulties (e.g. social isolation, lack of social/ language skills, deafness);
- persecutory delusions leading to hostility;
- delusional interpretation secondary to the effects of loss of respect from others.

Possible cognitive explanations for delusions

- Tendency to jump to conclusions on a single piece of evidence.
- Social attribution theory – tendency to attribute negative events to external causes and positive events to self.
- Delusions as an adaptive response to factors triggering psychosis.

Other erroneous ideas

Over-valued idea

- acceptable and understandable ideas which become dominant and are pursued beyond the limits of reasonableness;
- usually associated with abnormal personality;
- e.g. morbid jealousy, dysmorphophobia, parasitophobia.

Content of delusions or other erroneous ideas

Paranoia

- paranoid – 'self-referent', includes persecutory, grandiose or other ideas referring to self;
- only describes the content; need to determine the form (e.g. delusion, over-valued ideas, etc.) for accurate diagnosis.

Persecution

- the commonest type of 'paranoid' delusions;
- the imagined 'persecutor' may be animate, inanimate or unknown;
- occurs in schizophrenia, depression, mania, organic states;
- persecutory over-valued ideas occur in some types of paranoid personality disorder.

Infidelity and jealousy

- unreasonable belief of their partner's unfaithfulness;
- may range from over-valued idea to delusion;

- may occur without other evidence of psychosis – often resistant to treatment and stable over time;
- often dependent on the partner;
- may *result* in partner's sexual involvement with others;
- may result in extreme violence or even homicide.

Love

Erotomania – delusions of loving and being loved.

Clerambault's syndrome – usually a woman believing (wrongly) that a man, usually of higher social status, is in love with her.

Misidentification

- *Capgras syndrome* – belief that a person (usually close to him) is replaced by an imposter;
- often associated with schizophrenia, manic-depressive psychosis and organic disorder;
- a form of delusional percept in schizophrenia;
- *Fregoli syndrome* – false identification of familiar people in strangers.

Grandiosity

- primary grandiose delusions (e.g. belief that one is famous);
- occurs in schizophrenia as a form of delusional intuition;
- secondary grandiose delusions (e.g. secondary to manic state).

Religion

- has become less common compared to past centuries;
- whether idea is delusional depends on the evidence given and how the belief is held;
- delusions may be secondary to schizophrenia, mania or depression.

Guilt and unworthiness

- usually secondary to depression;
- may lead to suicide or homicide (with the intention to 'help' others out).

Nihilism

- belief that the subject and the world have disappeared and died;
- mostly associated with depression.

Hypochondriasis

- negative beliefs relating to bodily functions;
- occurs in depression, schizophrenia, or delusional disorders.

Infestation

- e.g. Ekbom's syndrome;
- may occur in conditions associated with tactile hallucinations (e.g. delirium tremens);
- may lead to secondary tactile hallucination;
- may be a form of monosymptomatic hypochondriacal psychosis.

Shared delusions
- Folie à deux – usually a dominant person and an associate;
- separation results in remission of symptoms in the associate;
- associate is usually disadvantaged (e.g. socially, physically).

Disorders in thinking

Types of thinking

Fantasy thinking – undirected. May be used to deny painful external reality.
Imaginative thinking – the use of spontaneous ideas in a constructive manner.
Rational thinking – logical ways to solve problems.

Examples of disordered thinking

Jasper's model of associative thinking:
- Thoughts flow by, one thought triggering (association with) the next.
- In each association, there are several possible thoughts (*constellation*) but one is actually chosen.
- Determining tendency – control of the final goal in the flow of thoughts.

Accelerated thought (flight of ideas)
- logical association – i.e. logical connection between one thought and the next;
- weak determining tendency – i.e. goal of thoughts not maintained due to rapid association formation and high distractibility;
- typical in mania.

Retarded thought
- slow association formation, though logical;
- usually pre-occupation with pessimistic thoughts;
- manifest in difficulty in concentrating and making decisions;
- typically occurs in depression;
- may be associated with motor agitation (e.g. in mixed affective states).

Thought interruption
Derailment
- Breakdown of connection between one thought and another.
- Thoughts not goal-directed.
- Occurs in schizophrenia.

Fusion
- Illogical linking of two unrelated thoughts.
- Limited goal-directed nature of thoughts.
- Occurs in schizophrenia.

Drivelling
- Extreme degrees of derailment and fusion.
- Completely illogical thoughts and incomprehensible speech.

Thought blocking
- Unexpected and unexplained breaking off during a chain of thought.
- Occurs in schizophrenia.
- Different from thought withdrawal (feeling of thoughts taken out by others).

Circumstantial thinking
- Slow progression towards the goal due to inability to distinguish between figure (important theme) from ground (background).
- Logical connection between thoughts.
- Goal is reached (though takes a long time).
- Seen in epilepsy, organic disorders, mental retardation.

Other abnormal thoughts associated with schizophrenia

Concrete thinking
- Literal interpretation and understanding of metaphorical expressions.
- Typically seen in schizophrenia.
- Useful to distinguish between schizophrenia and strong religious beliefs.

Over-inclusive thinking
- Tendency to include items which are only remotely relevant into the stream of thoughts.
- Inability to preserve conceptual boundaries.
- Assessed by sorting tests.

Applications of personal construct theory

- Unreliable construction of people and objects.
- Measured by repertory grid.
- *Schizophrenic inattention*
  - Inability to filter out irrelevant sensory data.
  - Tendency to 'lose one's thread' in speech and difficulty in completing a task.

Delusions of control of thoughts
Passivity of thoughts

- Attributes one's own internal thoughts to outside influences.
- Failure to discriminate between thoughts of the self and those of the outside world.
- Various forms – all first-rank symptoms of schizophrenia:
  thought insertion – thoughts brought in from outside oneself;
  thought withdrawal – thoughts taken away against one's will;
  thought broadcasting – thoughts diffuse widely to outside world beyond one's control;

First-rank symptoms of schizophrenia
Presence makes diagnosis more likely, but absence does not exclude it. Symptoms include:

Passivity of thought – thought withdrawal, insertion and broadcasting.
Other passivity experience – 'made' feelings, drives, or volition.
Somatic experience – delusion of control of parts of the body.
Auditory hallucinations – audible thoughts, running commentary, voices discussing the patient.
Delusional percept.

Descriptive terms in language and speech disorders

Aphonia – loss of ability to vocalise; due to neurological disorders or hysteria.
Dysphonia – impairment of vocalisation.
Dysarthria – disorders of articulation.
Logoclonia – spastic repetition of syllables (e.g. in Parkinson's disease).
Echolalia – repetition of words spoken by others; occurs in organic states, schizophrenia and mental retardation.
Word salad – recognisable words arranged in meaningless manner due to lack of syntax; occurs in schizophrenia.
Mutism – refusal to speak despite being conscious. Occurs in a wide range of conditions; e.g. organic disorders, drugs, catatonic schizophrenia, depression, and personality disorders.

Neurological basis of language disorders

- Handedness and localisation of speech centres:

Right-handed – speech function localised in the left hemisphere in
> 90% of people.
Left-handed/ambidextrous – mostly localised in the left hemisphere, rest in
right or bilateral representation.

- Brain structures and major types of dysphasia:

	Sensory dysphasia		Motor dysphasia
	Receptive	Conductive	Expressive
Neurological damage	Wernicke's area (auditory association area)	Pathway between Wernicke's and Broca's area	Broca's area (motorassociation area)
Spontaneous speech	Fluent	Fluent	Hesitant, slow, difficulty in selecting words
Comprehension of speech	Unable to understand	Able to understand	Able to understand
Repetition of message	Unable	Unable	Able

Language disorders in schizophrenia

Reflecting underlying thought disorder – e.g. loss of continuity of association,
over-inclusive thinking, concrete thinking, derailment, poverty of
thought, tangentiality, etc.
Private symbolism – includes use of new words *(neologism)*, existing stock
words/phrases with private meanings (either in speech *(cryptolalia)* or
writing *(cryptographia)*).
Misuse of words/phrases:

Inappropriate associations – inability to distinguish the associative
meanings of words (e.g. 'evil' is different from 'bad' and has a moral
dimension).
Inappropriate intrusion of dominant meaning – e.g. the word 'hand' has a
dominant meaning describing a part of the body, as well as meanings
in other context as in 'hand in an assignment'. In schizophrenia, the
dominant meaning may intrude inappropriately.

Inappropriate grammatical structure:
  Paralogia – intrusion of irrelevant thought.
  Paraphasia – words destroyed by meaningless interpolations.
  Literal paraphasia – misuse of the meanings of words.
  Paragrammatism – sentences with complicated clauses, reflecting circumstantial thinking.

Disorders of self

Elements of the feeling of self

- Activity (i.e. awareness that one is doing something).
- Unity (i.e. a single person).
- Identity (knowing 'who am I?').
- Boundary.

Disorders of feeling of unity

Autoscopy (phantom mirror image)
- Experience of seeing oneself and being convinced that the image is himself.
- Associated with the feeling of loss of familiarity with oneself.
- May involve other modes of perception.

Doppelganger (the double phenomenon)
- The subjective feeling that one is both outside and inside oneself.
- The 'double' may be perceptual, delusional, or due to depersonalisation.
- May occur in organic states, delirium, schizophrenia, fantasy.

Multiple personality

- An outside observer sees more than one personality manifested by the same person at different times.
- Each 'personality' claims to have no knowledge or memory of the others.
- Sometimes, one personality may know and remember the second, but not vice versa.

Disorders of identity

- A subjective feeling of loss of continuity of self.
- May occur in schizophrenia, neuroses, personality disorders, and in health.
- Intensity varies from delusion (in psychosis) to having good insight (in health).

Possession state

- A belief that one is possessed (e.g. by a dead relative).
- Occurs under a trance or altered state of consciousness.
- Usually associated with dissociative disorder, but may occur in normal people (e.g. during a trance or mass hysteria).
- Distinction from a normal state within a cultural or religious context:
  - unwanted,
  - distress to individuals,
  - prolonged beyond immediate triggering events.

Loss of boundaries of self

- Disturbed in schizophrenia, drug misuse.
- Most first-rank symptoms denote this loss of boundaries.

Depersonalisation

- The subjective unpleasant experience *as if* the individual were unreal.
- Usually associated with a change in mood (e.g. feeling detached, hollow, 'not oneself').
- May be associated with a distorted time sense.
- May occur in attacks lasting from seconds to months.
- Occurs in a wide variety of conditions: healthy subjects, sleep deprivation, organic disorder (e.g. temporal lobe epilepsy), depression, phobic anxiety, hysterical dissociation, alcohol and drug misuse, post-traumatic stress disorder.
- More likely in individuals with certain personalities (e.g. obsessional personality).
- Often associated with derealisation – the subjective unpleasant experience that the outside world is unreal.
- Blurring of boundary between ego and the external world.

Hypochondriacal disorders

- *Content*: Subjective awareness resulting in a person taking excessive account of his symptoms.
- *Forms*:
  - hallucinations (e.g. hearing voices saying 'you have AIDS');
  - primary or secondary delusions, or over-valued idea;

- obsessive and depressive ruminations;
- anxious preoccupation.
- Numerous modes of expression: e.g. pain, fear of illness, etc.
- Possible mechanisms:
  - misinterpretation of normal physiological sensation;
  - conversion of unwanted affect into physical symptoms;
  - mood disorder leading to changes in autonomic nervous system.
- Mood disorders presenting as somatic symptoms are common in certain cultures (e.g. Indian subcontinent, South East Asia, West Indies), perhaps due to psychological symptoms not widely accepted socially.
- Common bodily symptoms involved: headaches, gastrointestinal (e.g. constipation, indigestion, abdominal pain), musculoskeletal (e.g. aches and pains).
- May be secondary to a wide variety of conditions: depression, anxiety, schizophrenia.
- May co-exist with a physical disorder.

Dissociative disorders

- For both conversion and dissociative disorders, there are unconscious psychogenic symptoms which confer advantages (i.e. secondary gain) on the patient.
- In dissociation, there is a narrowing of the field of consciousness with amnesia (i.e. psychological symptoms, e.g., in fugue).
- In conversion, physical illness with no organic pathology results.
- A significant proportion of patients with the disorder subsequently develop other psychiatric or organic disorders.

Artefactual illness, dysmorphophobia, eating disorders

Artefactual illness

Illness or complaints produced by the individual himself/herself.
Factitious disorder – symptoms deliberately simulated or produced by the individual (e.g., in order to maintain a sick role, but not for external incentives).

Munchausen syndrome – chronic factitious disorder with physical symptoms (usually present with multiple admissions to hospitals).
Malingering – symptoms deliberately simulated or produced by the individual for recognisable external motives (e.g. compensation).

Dysmorphophobia

- Subjective feeling of the presence of physical defect which the individual considers noticeable by others, although objective appearance is within normal limits.
- A significant proportion suffer from a personality disorder.
- May take the form of an over-valued idea or delusion. May occasionally develop into schizophrenia.
- Surgery may reduce the psychiatric symptoms.

Eating disorders

Anorexia nervosa

- Characterised by
  - low body weight ($>15\%$ below expected);
  - self-induced weight loss due to dread of fatness as an intrusive over-valued idea;
  - body-image distortion;
  - widespread endocrine disorder, with probable delayed puberty.
- Linked to social cultures perceiving thinness as a requirement of beauty (e.g. UK), rare in African countries.
- Gross overestimation of their body size.
- Fear of loss of control not confined to eating. May be associated with other obsessional symptoms.

Bulimia nervosa

- Features
  - Morbid dread of fatness which makes the individual set a weight threshold below the optimum.
  - Persistent preoccupation with eating.
  - An irresistible craving for food which the patient occasionally succumbs to with bouts of overeating.
  - Attempts to counteract effects of overeating (e.g. self-induced vomiting, abuse of purgatives).
- Often a past history of anorexia nervosa
- May be associated with depression and guilt feelings

Affect and emotional disorders

Pathological changes in mood

Kraeplin's triad

Three components associated with mood:

- Abnormal mood (e.g. reduced in depression, elation in mania).
- Psychic activity (e.g. reduced in retarded depression, flights of ideas in mania).
- Motor activity (e.g. reduced in retarded depression, over-activity in agitated depression or mania).

  It is possible to be over-active in one component and underactive in another (e.g. mixed affective states).

Reduction in feelings

Apathy – absence of feelings, often associated with loss of energy and volition.

Blunting of affect – lack of emotional sensitivity.

Flattening of affect – restriction in the range of emotion.

All three states can be seen in schizophrenia.

Feeling of a loss of feeling

- Seen in depression, personality disorders and schizophrenia.

Anhedonia

- Inability to experience pleasure.
- One component of 'feeling of a loss of feeling'.
- Characteristic in depression, also seen in schizophrenia.

Feelings of capacity

- Helplessness and hopelessness – seen in psychotic depression.
- Increased feelings of capacity – seen in mania.

Heightened states of happiness

- *Ecstasy*
  - exalted state of happiness, usually self-referent with a loss of distinction of ego boundaries (e.g. feeling that one is merged with the world);
  - seen in organic states, schizophrenia, mania, dissociation disorders, mass hysteria.

- *Euphoria*
  - state of excessive and unreasonable cheerfulness;
  - seen in mania, organic states, damage to frontal lobe.

Mood changes and body feelings

- Changes in mood may result in
  - reduction in vitality,
  - physical symptoms (e.g. hypochondriasis).

Vital feelings

- *Vital self* – relationship between body and awareness of self.
- *Vital feelings* – feelings which make us aware of our vital self.
- *Coenestopathic states* – deep and constant awareness that we have of our bodies and the general tone of functional activity.
- In depression, global lowering of vitality involving all functions and performances; e.g. 'I am dead', 'like a band on my head' etc.

Religious feelings

- Difference between religious feelings and those associated with psychiatric disorders: The *form* is different, although the content may be similar.
- Indicators pointing feelings of apparent religious nature to a psychiatric illness:
  - other symptoms of mental illness;
  - lifestyle and direction of personal goal point towards history of mental illness;
  - disordered personality;
  - lack of reticence to discuss the experience with those likely to be sympathetic;
  - described in a matter-of-fact manner;
  - *inability to empathise with other's reservation to believe the experience*;
  - no implication that the experience will place a demand on the individual;
  - experience incongruent with the religious traditions relevant for the patient.

Depressive mood

- Anhedonia – see above.
- Retardation – slowing down of thoughts and action.

- Agitation in agitated depression, reflecting internal restlessness.
- Impairment of concentration by gloomy thoughts.
- Feeling of guilt and unworthiness.
- Delusions.
- Suicidal thoughts – actual suicide risk higher if agitation is present. Suicide often preceded by a period of apparent tranquillity.
- Homicidal thoughts – in order to save those close to the patient from the perceived intolerable world.

Loss and grief

Normal stages of grief
- Shock and numbness, probably a depersonalisation experience.
- Denial.
- Anxious searching (e.g. pseudohallucinations of bereavement).
- Depression and acceptance.

Morbid grief
- Phobic avoidance of any places, persons or things related to the deceased.
- Extreme guilt and anger about the deceased and the death.
- Physical illness.
- Recurrent nightmares about the deceased.

Mania

- *Elated mood.*
- *Accelerated thinking*:
  - increased distractibility and irritability;
  - flight of ideas with pressure of speech;
  - clang associations;
  - mood-congruent delusions (e.g. grandiose delusions).
- *Usually motor over-activity.*

Mixed affective states
Incongruence between motor activity, psychic activity, and mood states. Examples:

Agitated depression – motor over-activity but depressed mood and reduced psychic activity.
Manic stupor – elated mood, psychic over-activity, but in stupor.

Neurotic disorder

Anxiety

- May range from normal adaptive emotion to pathological state.
- State and trait:
  Anxiety state – the current experience of being anxious.
  Anxiety trait – the tendency to become anxious over a long period of time.
- Anxiety states may be provoked by very specific objects (e.g. situational anxiety) or not (i.e. free-floating anxiety).
- Main feature: constriction of the field of conscious awareness.
- Components of symptoms: somatic/autonomic and psychological, which usually (but not necessarily) correlate in intensity:
  Somatic/autonomic – e.g. dry mouth, palpitations, hyperventilation and dizziness, sweating, tremor, etc.
  Psychological – inability to relax, feeling of impending threat, anxious anticipation, exaggerated worries.

Panic disorders

- Attacks of marked psychic anxiety and fear associated with somatic and/ or autonomic symptoms.
- Usually an identifiable precipitating event exists which the subject tries hard to avoid.
- May last from minutes to hours, and may occur many times a day.

Phobias

- Fears which
  - are unreasonable and unexplainable;
  - are involuntary;
  - lead to avoidance of the feared object or situation.
- May be due to external stimuli (e.g. agoraphobia, social phobia, animal phobia) or internal stimuli (e.g. illness).

Obsessions and compulsions

Obsessions – recurrent *thoughts* which the subject knows to be his own and which the subject tries to resist but fails.
Compulsions – obsessions which are acted out.

Movement disorders in psychiatry

Over-activity

Agitation: Physical restlessness and exaggerated arousal reflecting a *subjective* mood state; seen in a wide range of disorders, including physical illness (e.g. hypothyroidism, organic states, schizophrenia, agitated depression, Alzheimer's dementia, etc.).

Hyperactivity: Objective increased motor activity, possibly associated with aggression and being over-talkative.

Retardation

• Slowness in initiating, performing and completing motor tasks.
• Often associated with retarded thinking (e.g. retarded depression), though not necessarily so (e.g. manic stupor).
• *Akinesis* – absence of voluntary movement.
• *Stupor* – absence of voluntary movement and speech (e.g. in severe depression, manic stupor, catatonic schizophrenia).

Movement disorders due to schizophrenia

Catatonia – greatly increased resting tone of muscles, but normal tone during voluntary movements; may be associated with stupor.

Waxy flexibility – maintaining posture of limbs placed by the examiner for a prolonged period of time.

Stereotypy – non-goal directed and repetitive movements.

Negativism – apparently resisting and opposing the examiner's request.

Aversion – turning away when the examiner addresses the patient.

Opposition – negative responses to different approaches by the examiner (e.g. verbal request, non-verbal attempt to make contact).

Automatic obedience – excessive compliance with examiner's instructions.

Advertence – turning towards examiner in an exaggerated manner when addressed.

Ambitendence – alternating between negativism and automatic obedience.

Forced grasping – inability to obey verbal requests not to perform an action (e.g. shaking the examiner's hand) which the examiner invites non-verbally (e.g. by presenting his hand).

Mitgehen (i.e. to go with) – moving limbs in the direction which the examiner initiated.

Echopraxia – imitating the examiner's actions.

Movement disorders caused by neuroleptic drugs

Parkinsonian symptoms – e.g. resting tremor, cogwheel rigidity, brady-kinesia, abnormal gait (e.g. failure to swing arm, difficulty in initiation).
Akathisia – motor restlessness especially of the legs, often associated with subjective feeling of not being able to sit still.
Acute dystonia – abnormal posture caused by sustained muscular contraction, affecting especially the head, neck, and limbs. Includes oculogyric crisis. Requires urgent treatment.
Tardive dyskinesia – purposeless, repetitive movements of the face, mouth, and tongue. The relative contribution of the natural history of schizophrenia and drug is unclear.

Psychoanalytic theories

Freud

- Born 1856 in Vienna; Psychiatrist at University of Vienna; died 1939 in England.
- Collaborated with Breuer in early years on the treatment of hysteria by hypnosis.
- First to view neurotic behaviour as goal-directed, and not merely as a physiological abnormality.
- Established classical psychoanalytical theory.

Structure of the mind

Three zones with different levels of reflective self-awareness:

The conscious – the part which includes all that one is momentarily aware of.
The preconscious – emotions or knowledge not momentarily in conscious-ness but are easily accessible.
The unconscious – contains repressed desires or childhood experiences that are too threatening or painful to be accepted into consciousness (e.g. too immoral).
The unconscious also accommodates principles governing what material should be repressed *(laws of transformation)*. However, repressed material in the unconscious may manifest in disguised form as neurotic symptoms. Hence, the unconscious may hold information which may explain adult behaviour in terms of childhood experience. This forms the basis of psychoanalysis using free association.

The id, ego and superego

Freud divided the mind into three sets of *functions*:- id, ego and superego.

Id (i.e. 'it-like')
- the primitive, biological, and instinctive drive demanding immediate gratification;
- tends to be destructive;
- governed entirely by *primary process* (e.g. the pleasure principle, irrational).

Ego (i.e. 'I')
- cluster of cognitions and perceptions which are in touch with reality (e.g. memory, problem-solving);
- contains specific defence mechanisms to transform the demands by the id and the prohibitions by the superego into terms manageable and reconcilable with reality, and thus maintaining psychic balance.
- governed by *secondary process* (i.e. conscious, logical, using reality principle).

Superego
- internalised ethical and moral codes of conduct;
- responsible for self-imposed standard of morals;
- unconsciously sought punishment for transgression, hence inducing guilt feelings.

Process of development

Pre-Oedipal stages

- Instincts – natural tendency to satisfy biological needs (e.g. food).
- Besides satisfying biological needs, 'sexual pleasure' may also be derived from this activity (e.g. sucking mother's breasts).
- Sexual drive gradually develops separately from its original biological function.
- Different *erotogenic zones* discovered in different stages of child development.
- Same process occurs for both males and females in the pre-Oedipal stages.
- 3 stages
  Oral stage – e.g. constantly putting objects into the mouth.
  Anal stage – derives pleasure from defecation; desire for retention and possessive control (e.g. during toilet training); described by Freud as 'sadistic'.

Phallic stage – focused on genitals.
● The 3 stages overlap to some extent.

Oedipal stages

● *Boy*
  1. Strongly desires to unite with mother.
  2. Comes to realise that females are 'castrated'.
  3. Develops fear of castration if he does not abandon his desire for mother.
  4. Hence represses desires and identifies with father.
  5. Oedipal complex resolved and adopts masculine role.
● *Girl*
  1. Attaches to mother (i.e. homosexual desire).
  2. Comes to realise that she is 'castrated' and hence inferior.
  3. Discovers that mother is also 'castrated' and inferior.
  4. Tries to abandon mother and seduce father.
  5. Fails to seduce father and identifies with mother.
  6. Oedipal (or Electra) complex resolved and adopts feminine role.

Responses to adversity

● *Repression* of painful experiences into the unconscious – theory initiated by Freud's experience during the treatment of 'Anna O' of hysteria. Repressed material may be recovered by free association or in dreams.
● Failure to progress in the pre-Oedipal stages – e.g. 'stuck' in oral phases in patients with alcohol problems; anal phases for patients with obsessive compulsive disorder, etc.
● Failure to resolve Oedipal complex.

Jung

● Born 1875 in Switzerland; psychiatrist; met Freud in 1907 in Vienna; died 1961.
● Shared some aspects of Freud's views, but also disagreed with Freud on many issues.

Structure of the mind
3 parts

● *Ego* – the conscious mind.
● *Personal unconscious* – elements not currently conscious though capable of being conscious.

- *Collective unconscious* – a pool of psychic knowledge and experience we inherit and are born with that constantly influences our behaviour; e.g. falling in love, creative arts, spiritual experiences.

Archetypes

- Innate tendency to experience events in specific ways.
- Form the contents of the collective unconscious. Examples of archetypes include:
  Mother archetype (an example of archetype) – innate tendency to want a mother or mother-substitute.
  Mana – spiritual power.
  Shadow – prehuman animal 'dark side' of our ego. (e.g. violence, death).
  Persona – public image, maybe our false selves.
  Syzygy – consists of:
  Anima – the female aspect present in the collective unconscious of men.
  Animus – the male aspect present in the collective unconscious of women.
- Important for much of love life

How the structure operates

Principles of opposites

- Every wish automatically suggests its opposite.
- The contrast creates the libido of the psyche.

Principle of equivalence

- Energy created is transmitted to both sides equally.
- Acknowledgement of the other (evil) wish results in personal growth.
- Denial results in the development of a complex – pattern of suppressed thoughts and feelings around a theme of some archetype.

Principle of entropy

- Tendency for oppositions to come together and decrease the energy over a person's lifetime; e.g., as we grow older, we tend to be less extreme and idealistic, and see both sides of ourselves (i.e. *transcendence*).
- *Self* – archetype representing both sides of all opposites; i.e. neither one extreme or nor the other.
- Our main goal of life is to 'realise the self'.

Synchronicity

- Two events not causally linked but may be meaningfully related; e.g. a prophecy coming true.
- May indicate how humans and nature are linked through the collective unconscious.

Functions

We use different proportions of the following 4 basic ways (functions) of dealing with the world:

Sensing – using perception only.
Thinking – rational function.
Intuiting – irrational, but involving a complex process of integration of a large amount of information.
Feeling – emotional response.

Klein

- Born 1882, paediatrician, died 1960.
- Extended Freud's work, but with considerable differences regarding approaches in children.
- Based Object Relations Theory on play therapy and interpretative techniques in children – though Anna Freud considered the ego in children not sufficiently developed for analysis.
- Theory had been applied to adults with neurotic or psychotic symptoms.

Object relations theory

- Importance of human relationships in development of the self (e.g. relationship with mother in infancy).
- Psyche is constantly in a state of flux.
- In infancy – fantasy of destroying the maternal body, which leads to paranoid anxiety of being *annihilated* (i.e. fear of death).
- To cope with this anxiety, infant *projects* this death drive (and aggression) onto the outside world (e.g. mother's body).
- The mother's body, which now contains the projected bad parts, is seen to be threatening. This leads to fear of persecution.
- To avoid these destructive feelings, infants *split* the maternal body into good and bad parts:

'*Good*' *breast* – full of goodness and perfection, which the infant idealises.

'*Bad*' *breast* – death drive and reality giving rise to persecution fantasy and fears of annihilation, which the infant attacks.

- Defence mechanisms the infant uses to protect its fragile and fragmented ego:

  Projection – an intolerable feeling which the infant attributes to the external world (e.g. aggressive feeling).

  Projective identification – an intolerable aspect of the self placed outside, onto the mother.

  Introjective identification – taking good bits of the good breast into the self.

- *Paranoid–schizoid position*
  - the equivalence of pre-Oedipal stage, usually in the first 6 months of life;
  - characterised by the use of splitting to keep the idealised good breast away from the bad breast, and fear that the persecutory object would destroy both the good breast and the self;
  - splitting, projective identification, idealisation and omnipotence important;
  - these processes are important in the developing of the ego and superego.

- *Depressive position*
  - usually achieved in the second 6 months during the first year of life, equivalent to the Oedipal stage;
  - gradual shift from relations with split objects to whole objects;
  - introjection of the *whole* object – good and bad aspects of the mother are not seen as separate;
  - leads to feeling of guilt and depression, as aggressive feelings were previously directed towards the loved object.

Winnicott

- Born 1896; paediatrician; died 1971.
- Built on Klein's object relations theory.

Similarities and differences between Klein and Winnicott

Similarities
- Both stressed the importance of psychic life in the first few months of life.

- Both accepted introjection and projection as important mechanisms.
- Both gave importance to 'objects'.

Differences

- Winnicott did not accept primary aggressive instinct (i.e. 'death drive').
- Winnicott placed more importance on environment.

Winnicott's theory on healthy development

- Child's development depends critically on the relationship with a real influential parent.
- Mother must be a *'good enough mother'* to provide a *holding environment* to protect the infant from *primitive anxieties.*
- Mother's *'primary maternal preoccupation'* creates the *'illusion of omnipotence'* to the infant that it has created a loving object.
- This illusion will ultimately encourage creativity.
- However, creativity develops only if the right balance between fantasy and reality testing is maintained.
- Mother also provides for *disillusionment* without despair.
- Child constantly explores boundaries between inner and outer experiences.
- *Transitional objects* (e.g. a piece of cloth) open out a potential space between fantasy and reality, and ease the journey from total dependence to 'mature dependence'.
- These processes ensure that the child develops a *true self* – i.e. instinctive core of the personality.

Winnicott's theory on abnormal development

- False self may be created when mother fails to meet the infant's needs, leading to the true self feeling too threatened to reveal itself.
- False self constantly anticipates the reactions of others, and serves to protect the true self from attack.

Defence mechanisms

- Psychological mechanisms allowing unconscious but purposeful control processes to avoid fear-evoking themes from reaching consciousness.
- Classification of defence mechanisms can be arbitrary and depends on the degree to which they are used.

Primitive or immature defence mechanisms

Denial – avoiding painful external reality from reaching consciousness. This may be achieved by not understanding the meaning or the implications of what is perceived.

Distortion – altering the meaning and evaluations to distort the perception of a stressful event. Includes minimisation (i.e. undervaluing a topic); exaggeration; devaluation (i.e. attributing negative qualities to self or others); disavowal (i.e. asserting that a situation does not matter).

Idealisation – exaggerating positive qualities to others.

Omnipotent control – acting as if one has total control of the others (or even the environment), to defend against the stress of being abandoned by others. Common amongst doctors dealing with stressful clinical life-and-death situations.

Splitting/Projection/Projective identification – see Klein above.

Isolation – splitting of feelings (e.g. trying to be indifferent about an important person by 'killing off' any feelings towards the person).

Passive aggression – indirectly and unassertively expressing aggression towards others to deal with stress.

Regression – returning to earlier modes of dealing with the world (e.g. regressing to childlike behaviour when an adult is instituted in prison or hospital).

Somatisation – dealing with emotional conflicts by preoccupation with physical symptoms unaccounted for by any actual physical cause.

Turning against the self – inappropriate feeling towards others is redirected to oneself; e.g., attempt to use self-mutilation to deal with anger towards others.

Intermediate defence mechanisms

Repression – involuntarily withholding from conscious awareness a painful experience, idea or feeling to avoid emotional conflict

Intellectualisation – avoiding the emotional implications of an event or issue by tackling it on a purely intellectual level. Common amongst doctors in dealing with emotional scenarios in clinical situations.

Rationalisation – giving logical reasons to justify actions actually performed for other reasons (e.g. to avoid self-blame).

Reaction formation – Replacing a feeling or idea warded off the consciousness with its exact opposite; e.g., a person with aggressive impulse towards another may be obsessively kind to the person.

Common in obsessive–compulsive disorders.

Undoing – expressing both the impulse and its exact opposite. Common in obsessive–compulsive disorder.

Mature defence mechanisms

Altruism – dealing with emotional conflicts by committing oneself to fulfil the needs of others rather than one's own.

Sublimation – replacing an unacceptable wish with similar, more socially acceptable actions (e.g. aggression may be turned into useful work such as joining the army).

Suppression – voluntarily avoiding thinking about a painful experience, idea or feeling to avoid emotional conflicts.

Humour – dealing with emotional conflict by emphasising its ironic and amusing aspects.

Transference and counter-transference

Transference – displacement of feelings and attitudes applicable towards other persons (usually important developmental figures, e.g. parents) to current relationships.

Transference reaction – displacement of such feelings onto the therapist during therapy.

Negative transference reactions – unrealistic negative expectations of the therapist (e.g. expectation of hostility, uncaring).

Positive transference reactions – unrealistic positive expectations of the therapist (e.g. expectation of being perfect, loving); 'falling in love' with the therapist.

Maternal/paternal/sibling transference – unrealistic expectation of re-enactment of role–relationship models applicable to the mother, father, or sibling.

Pre-Oedipal transference – transference of themes related to the nurturing and control, but not sexual longing or rivalry.

Oedipal transference – transference of themes related to sexual longing, rivalry.

Idealising transference – unrealistic expectation of self-improvement from being associated with the 'great ideal therapist'.

Counter-transference reaction – the other person's (e.g. therapist) displacement of feelings and attitudes towards the patient.

4 | Psychopharmacology

General principles

Classification

There are many correct ways of classifying psychotropic drugs. One method is to divide them as follows:

Hypnotic and anxiolytic agents

- Benzodiazepines.
- 5-HT$_{1A}$-receptor agonists (e.g. buspirone).
- Barbiturates.
- β-adrenoceptor antagonists.
- Miscellaneous (e.g. chloral hydrate, antihistamines).

Antipsychotic agents

Typical antipsychotics
- Phenothiazines (e.g. chlorpromazine, thioridazine).
- Butyrophenones (e.g. haloperidol).
- Thioxanthines (e.g. flupentixol).

Atypical antipsychotics
- Dibenzodiazepine (e.g. clozapine).
- Benzamide (e.g. sulpride, remoxipride).
- Benzixazole (e.g. risperidone).

Drugs used in treating affective disorders
Mood-altering agents

- *Antidepressants*
  - tricyclics (e.g. imipramine, amitriptyline),
  - selective 5HT uptake inhibitors (e.g. fluoxetine, paroxetine),

- non-selective MAO inhibitors (e.g. phenelzine),
- selective MAO-A inhibitors (e.g. moclobemide),
- atypical antidepressants (e.g. mianserin, trazodone).
- *Mood stabilising agents*
  - lithium,
  - carbamazepine,
  - valproate.

Anti-epileptic agents

- Phenytoin.
- Carbamazepine.
- Valproate.
- Benzodiazepines.
- Barbiturates.
- Newer drugs (e.g. vigabatrin).

CNS stimulants

- Methylphenidate (for attention-deficit hyperactivity disorders in children).
- Dexamphetamine (for narcolepsy).

Drugs used for dementia

- Anticholinesterase inhibitors (e.g. donezepil, *rivastigmine*).

Drugs used for substance dependence

- GABA analogue (e.g. acamprosate for alcohol dependence).
- Aldehyde dehydrogenase inhibitors (e.g. disulfiram for alcohol dependence).
- Opioid agonists (e.g. methadone for opiate dependence).
- Opioid antagonists (e.g. Naltrexone for opiate dependence).

Optimising patients' compliance

Factors for poor compliance

- Prescription not dispensed.
- Prescription not collected.
- Purpose of medicine unclear to patients/relatives.
- Instructions of administration unclear.
- Perceived lack of efficacy.

- Real or perceived side-effects.
- Physical difficulty in taking medicines.
- Unattractive preparation (e.g. unpleasant taste).
- Complicated regimen.

Improving compliance

- Ensure medication is dispensed and collected (e.g. via community nurses, relatives).
- Explain clearly purposes and perceived health outcomes of medicine.
- Explain clearly how and when medicines should be taken.
- Explain potential side-effects appropriately.
- Reinforce instructions (e.g. by nurse, pharmacists, written material).
- Use simple regimes if possible (e.g. once daily, combined preparation, etc.).
- Use attractive formulation if possible.
- Monitor compliance continuously (e.g. ask relatives, check pills, drug levels, etc.).

Placebo effects

- *Placebo* – any inert treatment (e.g. dummy medication or treatment) deliberately used for non-specific psychological or psychophysiological effect.
- It was thought that a third of patients respond to placebo, although a recent systematic review found little evidence of placebo effects other than for treatment of pain.
- Placebo effect: due to subconscious interactions between the doctor, the treatment process, and the patient.
- Placebo effects are increased by:
  - suitable disease – e.g. for pain, nausea, depression, anxiety, phobia; less for acute conditions;
  - good relationship between patients and doctors.
- Gender, suggestibility, and intelligence appear unimportant.
- Mechanism unclear – may be related to release of endogenous endorphins.
- Clinical use of placebo is made difficult by ethical considerations and difficulty in identifying placebo reactors.
- Final effects of any medication are the sum of its pharmacological and placebo effects.
- Hence essential to compare a drug with a placebo before concluding that it is an effective treatment.

Rational prescribing of psychoactive drugs

- The drugs must be more effective than placebo (use evidence-based approach; BNF listed drugs).
- Use appropriate dosage and route of administration, applying principles of pharmacokinetics and taking into account the patient's physical characteristics (e.g. renal and liver functions).
- Do not use two drugs which act in the same way simultaneously.
- Use the least number of drugs for a given effect, minimise potential drug interactions.
- Carefully balance the potential benefits and harm (e.g. dependence).
- Use the cheaper drug unless the expensive drug has been shown to be superior.
- Monitor compliance of treatment before changing treatment.
- Regularly review the need for continuing the drug.

Pharmacokinetics

General principles

Essential processes before optimal levels of an oral drug can act on the brain and other target tissues:

1. Absorption of drug across the epithelium of gastro-intestinal tract.
2. Metabolised in the liver before reaching the systemic circulation.
3. Distribution of drugs in appropriate compartments.
4. Crossing of blood–brain barrier (for drugs which act on the brain).
5. Appropriate elimination rates by the kidney.

N.B. Intravenous drugs avoid steps 1 and 2.

Passage of a drug through cell membranes
Drugs need to pass through cell membranes during

- absorption across the gastro-intestinal tract,
- excretion in renal tubules,
- distribution into various body compartments.

Most drugs diffuse through lipid, although some pass via cell-mediated transport (e.g. levodopa).

Factors increasing diffusion across lipid

- Increased lipid solubility.
- pH:
  - The unionised form of the drug (but not ionised form) passes through lipid easily.
  - Unionised form of acidic drugs increases with low pH.
  - Unionised form of basic drugs increases with high pH.
  - If different compartments have different pH, *ion trapping* will occur in the compartment with high pH for acidic drugs, and in the compartment with low pH for basic drugs; e.g., aspirin is concentrated in the alkaline renal tubule compared to plasma, and in the plasma compared to the stomach.

Absorption of drugs across the gastro-intestinal tract

Factors which increase absorption:

- high lipid solubility;
- low pH for acidic drugs, high pH for basic drugs;
- low acidity or alkalinity – generally strongly acidic or alkaline drugs are absorbed poorly;
- moderate gastrointestinal motility;
- increased splanchnic blood flow;
- small particle size;
- Modified-release preparations – smooth the release of active drugs and allows increase of dose intervals;
- suitable physiochemical properties.

First-pass metabolism

- Liver and gut wall contain enzymes which metabolise drugs absorbed in the gut.
- Psychotropic drugs which undergo substantial first-pass metabolism: chlorpromazine, chlormethiazole, imipramine, levodopa, morphine.
- Consequences:
  - much larger doses needed when given orally compared to intravenously;
  - considerable variations in appropriate oral doses amongst individuals, due to varying first-pass metabolism.

Metabolism by P450 enzymes

- Drug metabolism in the liver usually undergoes phase 1 reaction (oxidation, reduction, or hydrolysis) and phase 2 reactions (usually conjugation and inactivation).
- Many liver drug-metabolising enzymes (including cytochrome P450) are in the smooth endoplasmic reticulum.
- Cytochrome P450 enzymes have unique redox properties, and exhibit considerable genetic variations (which explains individual variations).
- SSRIs inhibit CYP2D6 enzymes. Hence, tricyclic antidepressant levels increase up to 3-fold if used simultaneously with SSRIs.

Distribution of drugs in various body compartments

Main body compartments (and percentage of body weight):

- intracellular water ($\sim$40%);
- extracellular fluid (consisting of plasma 5%; interstitial water 18%);
- fat ($\sim$20%).

Apparent volume of distribution (V_d)

- The volume of fluid which, at the same concentration as the plasma concentration, will contain the same amount of drug in the body.
- Formula: $V_d = $ Total amount of drug (Q)/plasma concentration (C_p).
- Hence, in a 70-kg person, V_d of drugs which are
  - confined to plasma compartment is about 3.5 litres;
  - confined to extracellular fluid is about 14 litres;
  - distributed amongst total body water is about 42 litres;
  - distributed amongst total body water and fat is over 42 litres.

Factors determining distribution of drugs amongst body compartments

Size of drug molecules – large drug molecules tend to be confined to the plasma component.

Binding to plasma protein

- drugs that bind strongly to plasma proteins tend to be confined to the plasma compartment; e.g. phenytoin.
- Hence, other drugs that compete for plasma proteins (e.g. phenobarbitone) may increase its plasma level. However, phenobarbitone also induces the hepatic metabolising enzymes and decreases its concentration. Hence, the resultant effect is unpredictable.

Lipid insolubility – lipid-insoluble drugs cannot pass cell membranes and hence tend to be confined to the extracellular compartment.

Lipid solubility – drugs that are highly lipid-soluble tend to distribute throughout the total body water (e.g. alcohol, phenytoin).

Binding to body fat

• drugs which are highly lipid-soluble and bind to body fat (e.g. tricyclic antidepressants, haloperidol, morphine).

• Practical implications: in overdose, difficult to be removed by haemodialysis.

Blood–brain barrier

• consists of a continuous layer of endothelial cells joined by tight junctions;

• drugs have effects on the brain only if they cross this barrier;

• factors determining permeability of drugs across this barrier:

Lipid solubility – lipid soluble drugs are permeable;

Chemoreceptor trigger zone areas – hence allows domperidone (anti-dopaminergic drugs) to be used for nausea;

Inflammation of meninges (e.g. meningitis) – hence penicillin is effective in treating meningitis;

Extreme stress – may cause barrier to be 'leaky'; explains how peripheral anticholinesterase inhibitor (e.g. pyridostigmine) causes central effects, as happened in the Gulf War.

• Practical implications:

– For example in the treatment of Parkinson's disease with levadopa, it is usually administered with a peripheral dopa decarboxylase inhibitor (e.g. benserazide);

– benserazide does not cross the blood–brain barrier;

– it inhibits the conversion of levadopa into dopamine in the periphery, but allows conversion centrally.

Renal excretion

Three processes:

Glomerular filtration – most drugs are freely filtered except those bound tightly to plasma proteins.

Active tubular secretion and reabsorption – e.g. dopamine, morphine, pethidine.

Passive diffusion across renal tubule

• drugs with high lipid solubility diffuse more easily and are excreted more slowly;

- basic drugs are excreted more rapidly in acid urine;
- acid drugs (e.g. salicylates) are excreted more rapidly in alkaline urine. Excretion rates are reduced in the elderly and in those with renal impairment. For drugs eliminated by kidneys (e.g. lithium), renal impairment leads to accumulation. Hence, there is a need to start with a low dose, increase it slowly, and monitor regularly.˙

Routes of administration

Oral
- may be poorly absorbed: poor lipid solubility, strong acids or bases;
- may undergo first-pass metabolism, hence poor bioavailability;
- effective doses vary greatly amongst individuals;
- relatively slow onset;
- less fluctuation in concentration and increased dose frequency (especially for modified-release preparation).

Sublingual (e.g. glyceryl trinitrate and buprenorphine (temgesic))
- rapid onset;
- bypass first-pass metabolism in the liver.

Rectal (e.g. rectal diazepam for status epilepticus)
- rapid onset, but absorption unreliable;
- useful if intravenous access difficult.

Intravenous (e.g. intravenous haloperidol or diazepam for rapid tranquillisation)
- reliable;
- very rapid onset of action;
- effects usually short-lasting;
- continuous intravenous infusion can ensure steady concentration;
- higher incidence of acute side-effects (e.g. hypotension for IV haloperidol).

Intramuscular
- onset intermediate between oral and intravenous;
- rate of absorption depends on site of injection (e.g. faster for gluteal injection) and local blood flow (increases with high blood flow, and decreases with circulatory failure).

Intramuscular depot (e.g. antipsychotic depot injection)
- drug is dissolved in fractionated oil;
- drug is injected deep intramuscularly at intervals of 1–4 weeks;

- drug diffuses slowly from the oil depot to the body water phase;
- correct injection technique (e.g. z-track technique) and rotation of injection sites essential;
- allow drug to be released evenly over a period of many weeks.
- *Advantages*: avoidance of first-pass metabolism, ensuring compliance.
- *Disadvantage*: not possible to stop drugs quickly in the presence of side-effects, patient has no control.

Single-compartment model, 1ˢᵗ order kinetics

Intravenous administration, single bolus
- The concentration at time t after a quantity Q of drug with volume of distribution V_d and clearance CL is injected into the circulation is

$$C(t) = C(0) \exp[(-CL/V_d)t],$$

where $C(0)$ is the initial plasma concentration at time 0; i.e. the concentration declines exponentially with time.
- The elimination rate is CL/V_d.
- Half-life $(t_{1/2})$ is
  - the time taken for the plasma concentration to reduce to half its value;
  - constant under this model $= \ln 2/$elimination rate.

Intravenous administration, continuous administration
- Plasma concentration approaches the steady state exponentially until it is reached.
- The half-time is equal to the half-life $(t_{1/2})$.

Intravenous administration, repeated dosages
- Steady-state concentration is approached, but with fluctuations before and after a dosage is given.
- The smaller and the more frequent the dosages, the smoother the plasma concentration.
- Given the same total dose over a time period, the exact dosage schedule does not affect the mean steady-state concentration or the time taken to achieve it.
- Generally speaking, steady-state concentration is achieved after about 3 plasma half-times.
- The narrower the therapeutic window is (i.e. the difference between therapeutic and toxic doses), the more frequent and smaller dose regime is needed.

Oral administration, repeated dosages
- This is equivalent to the intravenous model with an additional rate constant for absorption.
- Effects of oral compared with iv administration:
  - delayed peak concentration;
  - reduced peak concentration;
  - more prolonged action;
  - area under the concentration–time curve is the same assuming 100% bioavailability.

Saturation (zero-order kinetics)
- The rate of elimination is limited; e.g. elimination of alcohol (limited by the enzyme alcohol dehydrogenase) and phenytoin.
- Rate of elimination is constant (e.g. alcohol at 4 mmol/hour) irrespective of plasma concentration.
- Duration of action depends strongly on the dose taken.
- If drug is administered continuously or by repeated dosage at a rate above elimination, plasma concentration will continue to rise and never settle down to a steady-state concentration.

Special problems with the elderly

- Increased sensitivity to drugs.
- Reduced liver metabolism and renal excretion.
- Increased fat to lean body mass ratio.
- Liability to fall.
- Therefore more likely to suffer from drug accumulation and side-effects.
- Prescription guidelines
  - use drugs only when necessary;
  - use smallest possible effective doses, increase slowly if necessary;
  - use simple regimes;
  - review regularly for the need to continue medication.

Relationship between plasma drug level and therapeutic response

Theoretical relationship between receptor fractional occupancy and concentration

- Rectangular hyperbola relationship between fractional occupancy and concentration.

- Symmetrical sigmoid curve if fractional occupancy is plotted against log concentration (dose–response curve).

Experimentally observed response–concentration curve

- Generally similar to the theoretical dose–response above.
- Slight discrepancy may reflect a non-linear relationship between receptor occupancy and clinical response.

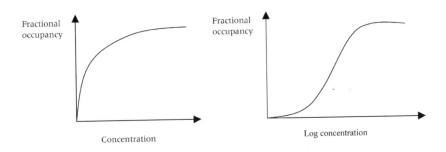

Measurement of toxicity

- In animal studies, LD_{50} (i.e. lethal dose, 50%) is the dose for which 50% of a group of subjects die.
- ED_{50} (i.e. effective dose, 50%) is the dose for which clinical effects are observed for 50% of subjects.
- Therapeutic index.
  Definition 1:

$$Therapeutic\ index = LD_{50}/ED_{50}$$

Critique:
ED_{50} depends on the clinical features concerned (e.g. for benzodiazepines, differs between anxiolytic or hypnotic properties).
LD_{50} only measures acute mortality, but not accumulated chronic side-effects.
Definition 2:

$$Therapeutic\ index = \frac{maximum\ non\text{-}toxic\ dose}{minimum\ effective\ dose}$$

Critique:
Individual variability is not taken into account.
- Therapeutic window – plasma concentrations between therapeutic and toxic doses.

Critique:
Difficult to define and measure these concentrations.

Lithium

- Relatively good relationship between drug level and clinical effects.
- Generally effective at a plasma concentration of 0.5–1 mmol/l, generally toxic above 1.5 mmol/l.
- Signs of toxicity: vomiting, diarrhoea at the earlier stages; polyuria, confusion, tremor, ataxia, convulsions, coma and death at high plasma concentrations. Hence, narrow therapeutic window
- Drugs in the body can be considered as being in 2 compartments: intracellular and extracellular:
  - extracellular lithium is excreted with a half-time of 12 hours;
  - intracellular drug is excreted over a longer period of time (about a week).
- Factors increasing toxicity:
  - renal impairment;
  - sodium depletion (as this increases renal reabsorption);
  - diuretic therapy.
  - old age.

Hence the need to regularly monitor plasma lithium level.

Antidepressants

- For tricyclic antidepressants, there are considerable individual variations between
  - the oral dose taken and the plasma level achieved (due to different metabolism by P450 enzymes and elimination);
  - the relationship between plasma level achieved and clinical effects.
- One study showed that antidepressant effect of nortriptyline is optimal between 200 and 400 nmol/l, but declines at higher levels.
- The general approach is to increase the dose gradually to the average therapeutic dose of tricyclic antidepressants daily for over 4 weeks.

- Due to considerable individual variations, the plasma level of tricyclic antidepressants is measured only if higher doses are used in the treatment of resistant depression.
- Plasma concentrations of other antidepressants are seldom measured.

Anti-epileptics

Phenytoin
- Therapeutic plasma concentration is narrow (about 40–100 μmol/l).
- Toxic effects (vertigo, ataxia, nystagmus, headache, confusion) may be severe above 150 μmol/l.
- At the therapeutic range, the metabolism of phenytoin displays saturation (zero-order) kinetics. A small increase (e.g. 50%) in dose may result in a large increase (e.g. up to 4-fold) in steady-state concentration.
- Hence, there will be considerable individual variation between dose taken and plasma level achieved, and it needs to be adjusted precisely.
- Plasma half-life (usually about 24 hours) increases with increasing dose of phenytoin.
- Monitoring of plasma level is essential.

Other anti-epileptics
- Relatively fewer toxic side-effects with carbamazepine, valproate and ethosuximide.
- Therapeutic range may vary amongst individuals.
- Monitoring is not always carried out.

Pharmacodynamics

Synaptic receptors

- A receptor is a target of the cell which mediates between a chemical messenger (e.g. drugs, endogenous transmitters) and the resultant cell function.
- Synaptic receptors are on the post-synaptic cell membranes (e.g. n-Ach, GABA).
- Activation of the synaptic receptor may result in cellular actions by opening or closing of ion channels (coupling with G-protein).

Opening and closing of ion channels

- Mainly involved in fast synaptic transmission.

- Examples: nicotinic acetylcholine (Na^+ channel), $GABA_A$ (Cl^- channel), 5-HT_3, glutamate receptors.
- Nicotinic ACh receptors best studied:
  - 5 subunits (α_2, β, γ, δ) clustering around a central transmembrane pore;
  - 2 acetylcholine-binding sites in the extracellular portion of each of the α-units;
  - changes in the α-helices when acetylcholine molecules bind;
  - conformational changes resulting in opening of the sodium channels.

G-protein coupled receptors

- G-protein – mediates between receptor and several effectors; e.g. muscarinic Ach, adrenoceptors, neuropeptide, all 5-HT (except 5-HT_3) receptors.
- Possible effectors for G-protein:
  - cAMP system (e.g. β-adrenoceptor, opioid, dopamine receptors);
  - inositol phosphate (IP_3) (e.g. lithium blocks the recycling pathway);
  - ion channels.
- G-protein consists of 2 subunits (α, β, γ); α subunit couples with receptors, β subunit binds to target.
- Molecular variation in G protein results in specificity.

Drug binding to receptors

Affinity – tendency of an agent (e.g. drug) to bind to a receptor.

Efficacy – the ability of an agent to produce an effect once bound to the receptor.

Agonist – an agent (e.g. drug) which activates a receptor (i.e. full efficacy), binds preferentially to the activated state of the receptor.

Antagonist – an agent which combines with a receptor without causing activation (i.e. no efficacy).

Partial agonist – an agent which causes submaximal response when combined to the receptor (i.e. intermediate efficacy).

Inverse agonist

- binds preferentially to the inactivated state of the receptor;
- produces the opposite effects of an agonist.

- Antagonists reverse the effects of both agonists and inverse agonists;
- e.g. diazepam-binding inhibitor and some analogues of benzodiazepine on $GABA_A$ receptor).

Main receptor types relevant to psychiatry

Receptor types	Subtypes	Examples of drugs
Acetylcholines	Nicotinic (neuro-muscular junction)	• *Antagonists*, e.g. tubocurarine • *Depolarising antagonists*, e.g. suxamethonium
	Muscarinic	• *Antagonists*, e.g. atropine • *Central anticholinesterase inhibitors*, e.g. tacrine (used in dementia)
Adrenoceptors	β_1	• *Agonists*, e.g. noradrenaline • *Antagonists*, e.g. propranolol
	α	• *NA uptake inhibitors*, e.g. tricyclic antidepressants • *Increasers of NA availability*, e.g. MAO inhibitors
5-HT	$5\text{-}HT_1$ predominantly inhibitory, important for depression $5\text{-}HT_2$ predominantly excitatory	• *$5\text{-}HT_{1A}$ agonists*, e.g. buspirone • *SSRIs* - these increase the availability of 5-HT • *$5\text{-}HT_2$ agonists*, e.g. hallucinogenics
Histamines	H_1	• *H_1 antagonists*, e.g. promethazine causes drowsiness
Dopamines	D_1 D_2 (related to schizophrenia and Parkinsonian symptoms)	• Very few subtype-specific drugs • *Agonists*, e.g. dopamine, bromocriptine • *Antagonists*, e.g. antipsychotics
Opioids	μ (analgesic effects) δ κ (dysphoria)	• Very few subtype-specific drugs • *Agonists*, e.g. morphine, codeine • *Partial agonists*, e.g. nalorphine • *Antagonists*, e.g. naloxone

| GABA | GABA$_A$ (anxiolytic, hypnotic effects) | • *Agonists on modulatory (BDZ) sites, e.g.* benzodiazepines
• *Antagonists on modulatory sites, e.g.* flumazenil
• *GABA-transaminase inhibitors, e.g.* vigabatrin |
| | GABA$_B$ (muscular relaxation) | *Agonists, e.g.* Baclofen |

Phenomena of up- and down-regulation

- Prolonged exposure to an agonist may cause deactivation (e.g. acetylcholine receptors on *neuromuscular* junction) or reduction in the number of receptors (*down-regulation*).
- Down-regulation, a higher level of drug needed to achieve the same effect, accounts for the phenomenon of tolerance and dependence.
- Prolonged exposure to an antagonist may cause supersensitivity or an increase in the number of receptors (up-regulation).
- Up-regulation of dopamine receptors may explain tardive dyskinesia after prolonged treatment with antipsychotic drugs.

Principal CNS pharmacology of the main groups of drugs used in psychiatry

Antipsychotic agents

Dopamine overactivity hypothesis of schizophrenia

- Amphetamine releases dopamine and produces clinical features similar to schizophrenia.
- Dopamine antagonists (especially D$_2$ antagonists) are effective in treating schizophrenia, and clinical potency correlates with affinity of D$_2$ receptors.
- Increase in dopamine receptors in limbic system found in schizophrenia.
- Although D$_2$ block is immediate, onset of antipsychotic effects occurs many weeks afterwards.
- Neurochemical studies were equivocal.
- Other receptors (e.g. 5-HT, histamine, α-adrenergic, glutamate) may also be important.

Main types of antipsychotic drugs

Typical (classical) antipsychotics

- Useful both for acute phase and relapse prevention.
- Include phenothiazines (e.g. chlorpromazine), butyrophenones (e.g. haloperidol) and thiozanthines (e.g. flupentixol).
- Introduced before 1980s.
- Act mainly by blocking mesolimbic dopamine receptors (mainly D_2, but also D_1).
- Mainly effective in treating positive symptoms.

Atypical antipsychotics

There include benzamides (e.g. sulpride), dibenzodiazepines (e.g. clozapine) and benzixazoles (e.g. risperidone). Initially, it was thought that compared with newer atypical drugs, atypical antipsychotic drugs

- have less extrapyramidal effects;
- are more effective against negative symptoms;
- are effective in treating patients not responding to classical drugs ('treatment-resistant').

However, a recent systematic review showed that, compared to classical antipsychotics, atypical psychotics

- have similar effects on symptoms;
- have fewer extrapyramidal side effects, but overall tolerability similar to conventional drugs.

Clozapine is thought to be effective in treating 30–50% of 'treatment-resistant' schizophrenia. It has a low D blocking effect, and may act via blocking $5\text{-}HT_2$ or D_4 receptors.

Main side-effects

- Extrapyramidal side-effects (EPS)
  Parkinsonian symptoms – due to D_2-receptor blockade in dopaminergic nigro-striatal pathway.
  Tardive dyskinesia – involuntary movements of the face and tongue; develops after months or years in about 30% of patients treated with classical antipsychotic drugs; may be due to increase in D receptor sites in the striatum.

- Endocrine effects
  - mainly due to D blockade of dopaminergic neurones in the pituitary, with resultant increase in prolactin secretion;
  - symptoms include breast swelling and lactation.
- Sedation – due to H_1 blocking effects.
- Hypotension – due to blockade of α-adrenoceptors.
- Antimuscarinic effects – e.g., dry mouth, blurred vision, etc.
- Neuroleptic malignant syndrome (NMS)
  - hyperthermia, mental confusion, muscular rigidity, labile blood pressure, tachycardia, sweating, increase in CPK;
  - much less common with atypical antipsychotics;
  - fatality rate 15%;
  - must stop neuroleptics immediately;
  - bromocriptine and dantrolene have been used for treatment.
- Clozapine may cause agranulocytosis (with resultant severe infections) as a dangerous idiosyncratic reaction. Needs meticulous monitoring of differential white cell counts by Clozaril Patient Monitoring Service.

High dose antipsychotic medication (i.e. above BNF antipsychotic doses; 'chlorpromazine equivalents' of up to 1 g daily)

- Risks: sudden cardiac-related death; CNS toxicity (e.g. CNS and respiratory depression).
- Possible uses: initial acute treatment; long term treatment in treatment-resistant patients.
- Factors to be considered:
  - the diagnosis is correct;
  - plasma levels are therapeutic;
  - drug compliance ensured;
  - treatment duration adequate;
  - trial of reduced doses;
  - trial of alternative drug therapies (e.g. atypical antipsychotics, lithium).
- Precautions needed
  - multidisciplinary team discussion;
  - consideration of contra-indications (e.g. cardiac);
  - consideration of drug interactions (e.g. with tricyclics);

- ECG before treatment and every 1–3 months (e.g. to exclude prolonged QT interval);
- very slow increase of dose;
- regular monitoring of pulse, blood pressure, temperature;
- regular review of prescription;
- reduction in dose after 3 months if no improvements.

Antidepressants

Monoamine theory of depression

- Depression is due to a functional deficit of monamine neurotransmitters (e.g. noradrenaline, 5-HT).
- Mania is due to a functional excess of monamine neurotransmitters.
- Supporting evidence:
  - Tricyclic antidepressants block NA and 5-HT reuptake, and improve mood.
  - MAO inhibitors increase stores of NA and 5-HT, and improve mood.
  - ECT probably increases central responses to NA and 5-HT, and improves mood.
  - Reserpine reduces NA and 5-HT storage, and may cause depression.
  - Methyldopa inhibits NA synthesis, and may cause depression.
- Evidence against theory:
  - Cocaine and amphetamine inhibit NA reuptake, but have no effects on depressed patients.
  - Methysergide is a 5-HT antagonist, but has no effects on mood.
  - Biochemical studies on monoamine metabolism and post-synaptic receptors in depressed patients were inconclusive.
  - Antidepressants have immediate effects on monoamine transmission, but delayed clinical effects.

Tricyclic antidepressants

Actions and uses

- Mechanism of action: inhibit the uptake of amines by nerve terminals in CNS, by competing for the binding site of the carrier protein.
- Most tricyclics inhibit both NA and 5-HT neurones, and both are probably important.

- They are most effective for treating moderate to severe endogenous depression associated with psychomotor and physiological changes (e.g. loss of appetite and sleep disturbances).
- A delay of at least 2 weeks is necessary for clinical effects.
- Once-daily administration (usually at night to avoid day-time drowsiness) is usually adequate due to their long half-life.
- Non-sedating types (e.g. lofepramine, imipramine) are better for the withdrawn and apathetic patients; sedating types (e.g. amitriptyline, clomipramine) are better for agitated and anxious patients.
- Doses should be gradually increased to a therapeutic level before concluding that it is ineffective.
- Lower doses should be used for elderly patients.
- Other uses: nocturnal enuresis for children; phobic and obsessional states (for clomipramine).

Side-effects

Antimuscarinic effects – e.g. dry mouth, blurred vision, drowsiness, constipation, urinary retention. Especially for amitriptyline.
H_1 *block effects* – drowsiness and confusion.
Postural hypotension – due to effects on medullar vasomotor centre.
Inappropriate ADH secretion causing hyponatraemia – usually in the elderly.
Cardiac effects – arrhythmia and heart block, especially amitriptyline (hence dangerous in overdoses).
Convulsions – hence caution is needed in epileptic patients.

Important drug interactions

- Tricyclics must not be used with *MAOI*. Wait for at least 2 weeks (3 weeks for clomipramine or imipramine).
- Interact with many drugs (e.g. SSRIs, alcohol, cimetidine) as tricyclics are metabolised by many cytochrome P450 enzymes.
- Increased cardiovascular side-effects with terfenadine.

Withdrawal

Possible symptoms of withdrawal after regular administration for 8 or more weeks:

- nausea, vomiting, and anorexia, accompanied by headache,
- giddiness,

- insomnia,
- occasionally hypomania or panic-anxiety.

Dosage should be reduced gradually over a 4-week period.

Selective serotonin uptake inhibitors (SSRIs)

Actions and uses

- Mechanism of action: selectively inhibit the uptake of 5-HT (over NA) by nerve terminals in CNS. E.g. fluoxetine, fluvoxamine, paroxetine, sertraline and citalopram.
- Effectiveness: generally equally effective compared to tricyclic antidepressants.
- Side-effects: less drowsiness, antimuscarinic effects and cardiotoxic side-effects. Safer in overdoses than tricyclics. However, SSRIs may cause more gastrointestinal side-effects (e.g. nausea and vomiting).
- Direct cost: SSRIs are more expensive.
- A delay of at least 2 weeks necessary for clinical effects.
- Other uses: obsessive–compulsive disorders (all SSRIs); bulimia nervosa (fluoxetine); panic disorder (paroxetine and citalopram) and social phobia (paroxetine).

Side-effects

Gastrointestinal – e.g. nausea, vomiting, dyspepsia, abdominal pain, anorexia with weight loss.
Convulsions – caution in epileptic patients.
Sexual dysfunction – loss of libido and failure of orgasm.
Hypomania or mania – caution in bipolar patients possibly entering manic phase.
Inappropriate ADH secretion causing hyponatraemia – usually in the elderly.
Serotonin syndrome – rare syndrome with fever, muscle rigidity, agitation, cardiovascular collapse, sweating, diarrhoea, lack of coordination, tremor. May be confused with neuroleptic malignant syndrome.
Suicidal ideation – controversial whether this effect is real.

Important drug reaction

- SSRI should not be started within 2 weeks of stopping an MAOI.
- MAOI should not be started within 2 weeks of stopping SSRI (5 weeks for fluoxetine).

Withdrawal

Withdraw gradually – abrupt withdrawal may cause headache, nausea, paraesthesia, dizziness and anxiety.

Non-selective MAO inhibitors (MAOIs)

Actions and uses

- Monoamine oxidase – intracellular enzyme:
  Type A: main substrate 5-HT, inhibition responsible for antidepressant actions.
  Type B: main substrate phenylethylamine, inhibition responsible for anti-Parkinsonian effects of selegiline.
- MAO important for inactivating endogenous and ingested amines (e.g. tyramine in cheese).
- Mechanism of action of MAOI
  – irreversible inhibition of both types of monoamine oxidase;
  – hence rapid prolonged increase in brain 5-HT and NA in cytoplasm;
  – this causes leakage of these monoamines into synapse.
- Causes of 'cheese reaction':
  – tyramine and some drugs are normally destroyed by MAO;
  – under MAOI medication, ingestion of these substances causes large amounts of monoamines to be released in synapses;
  – this may result in severe hypertension or even intracranial haemorrhages.
  Food: cheese, pickled herring, broad bean pods, bovril, oxo, marmite, other meat or yeast extract or fermented soya bean extract, alcohol.
  Drugs: a wide range of drugs, e.g. ephedrine, pethidine, general anaethestics, etc. Tricyclics and SSRIs may aggravate these reactions.
- Main clinical use
  – phobic patients and depressed patients with atypical, hypochondriacal, or hysterical features;
  – patients refractory to treatment with other antidepressants.
- Main drugs: phenelzine, isocarboxazid, tranylcypromine (to be avoided due to stimulant effect).
- Delay of 3 weeks or more for clinical effects.

Side-effects

Severe hypertension with food or drugs – see 'cheese reaction' above.

Postural hypotension – due to accumulation of other amines (e.g. dopamine) in *peripheral* sympathetic nerve terminals and interference with noradrenaline transmission.

Excitement and agitation – especially tranylcypromine.

Hepatoceullar necrosis – rare side-effects especially with phenelzine.

Withdrawal

• Slow withdrawal particularly important for MAOIs.

Reversible MAO-A inhibitors (RIMA)

• Mechanism of actions: reversible inhibition of monoamine oxidase type A.
• Mainly moclobemide.
• Used for major depression and phobia as a second-line drug.
• Risk of drug interactions much less than irreversible MAOI, but precautions with food and drugs should still be taken.
• Should not be given with another antidepressant.
• Short duration of action: may start another type of antidepressant immediately after moclobemide is stopped.

Mood stabilisers

Lithium

Actions and uses

• *Uses*:
  – prophylaxis and treatment of mania;
  – prophylaxis of bipolar disorder;
  – prophylaxis of recurrent unipolar depression.
• *Mechanisms of action*: Not fully understood, but may involve
  – phosphatidyl inosityl (PI) pathway; inhibition of the regeneration of PI causes a depletion of membrane PI and accumulation of intracellular inositol phosphate, and inhibition of IP_3 formation;
  – reduced cyclic AMP production.

- Narrow therapeutic window and regular plasma level monitoring important (see **Pharmacokinetics** above).
- Takes about 2 weeks to reach steady-state concentration (limited by rate of uptake by cells). Hence, antipsychotics should be used in acute phase of mania.
- Most effective treatment for mania prophylaxis, usual first line treatment.
- May have specific antisuicidal effects in mania.

Side-effects

- Gastro-intestinal symptoms: anorexia, vomiting diarrhoea.
- Tremor, ataxia, lack of co-ordination.
- Renal effects: polyuria.
- Thyroid enlargement and hypothyroidism.
- Weight gain.

Acute toxicity

- Hyperreflexia,
- Convulsions,
- Confusion and coma,
- Oliguria,
- Circulatory failure.

Caution in prescription

- Regular plasma concentrations (every 3 months if stable).
- Monitor thyroid function.
- Avoid in renal and cardiac disease.
- Reduce dose if vomiting or diarrhoea occur.
- Avoid sodium depletion (e.g. concurrent diuretics).
- *Pregnancy* – use with caution in first trimester (risk of Ebstein anomaly) and third trimester (risks of neonatal goitre and neonatal lithium toxicity).

Withdrawal

- No evidence of the existence of 'lithium withdrawal syndrome'.
- However, risk of relapse greater if rapidly withdrawn. Hence, withdraw slowly.

Carbamazepine

• Uses (other than as anticonvulsants):
  – alternative prophylaxis of bipolar disorder when lithium is ineffective;
  – particularly effective in patients with rapid cycling manic-depressive illness (4 or more affective episodes per year).
• Frequently used in USA and increasingly in Europe.
• Mechanism of action: Unclear.
• Good evidence of effectiveness in prophylaxis of mania and bipolar depression.
• Little evidence yet for its acute efficacy in bipolar depression.

Sodium valproate
Uses (other than as anticonvulsants):

• not yet licensed;
• proven effects by RCTs in treating mania, but not bipolar depression.

Other potential mood-stabilisers
The following drugs are actively researched:

• lamotrigine,
• atypical antipsychotics (e.g. clozapine),
• ω-3 fatty acids.

Anxiolytic and hypnotic drugs

Benzodiazepines
Actions and uses

• Used to
  – induce sleep,
  – reduce anxiety,
  – treat or prevent convulsions,
  – reduce muscle tone and co-ordination.
• Mechanism of action:
  – bind to regulatory site at $GABA_A$ receptor;
  – facilitate opening of GABA-activated chloride channels;
  – hence produce inhibitory effects as GABA-ergic neurones mediate fast inhibitory synaptic responses.

- Diazepam binding sites (like $GABA_A$ receptors) are highest in cerebral cortex.
- It is uncertain whether an endogenous benzodiazepine-like mediator exists.
- 2 types of BDZ receptors: BDZ_1 (sedative and anxiolytic effects) and BDZ_2 (anticonvulsant and muscle-relaxant effects).
- Different benzodiazepines differ mostly in their pharamacokinetic properties.
- Hypnotic effects:
  - Loprazolam, lormetazepam, and temazepam act for a shorter time and have little hangover effects. However, withdrawal phenomenon is more common.
  - Nitrazepam, flunitrazepam, and flurazepam have prolonged effects and may accumulate.
- Anxiolytic effects:
  - Diazepam, alprazolam, bromazepam, chlordiazepoxide, clobazam, and clorazepate have sustained actions.
  - Lorazepam and *oxazepam* are shorter-acting but withdrawal phenomena are more common.
- Clonazepam has more anticonvulsant/muscle-relaxant effects than hypnotic/anxiolytic effects. Possibly due to BDZ_1 selectivity.
- Pharmacokinetics:
  - bind strongly to plasma proteins;
  - high lipid solubility – hence accumulate in body fat;
  - all metabolised, some metabolites (e.g. nordaepam) may be pharmacologically active;
  - overall duration of action ranges from < 6 hours (e.g. triazolam) to over 5 days (e.g. flurazepam).

Side-effects

- Drowsiness and confusion, greatly increased by alcohol intake.
- Amnesia – taken advantage of for use before surgery.
- Impaired skills and job performance (including driving).
- Paradoxical effects – an increase in talkativeness, anxiety, hostility and aggression.
- Tolerance (gradual increase in dose needed for given effects) and physical dependence (withdrawal symptoms if drug is withdrawn).
- Overdose – rarely causes life-threatening respiratory depression, can be reversed by flumazenil (benzodiazepine antagonist, actions last about 2 hours).

Withdrawal

- Abrupt withdrawal may cause
  - confusion,
  - toxic psychosis,
  - convulsions,
  - a condition resembling delirium tremens.
- Benzodiazepine withdrawal syndrome:
  - insomnia,
  - anxiety,
  - loss of appetite and weight,
  - tremor,
  - perceptual disturbances.
- Timing of benzodiazepine withdrawal syndrome:
  - long acting drugs – may take up to 3 weeks;
  - short-acting drugs – few hours.
- Withdrawal:
  - transfer patients to equivalent doses of diazepam;
  - reduce in steps of about one-eighth of the daily dose every fortnight.

Royal College of Psychiatrists Guidelines on use of benzodiazepines

As anxiolytics:
- to be prescribed primarily for the short-term relief of reducing anxiety;
- may also be prescribed in chronic treatment-resistant anxiety or established dependency;
- **not** to be prescribed regularly for longer than 1 month;
- ideally to be given on an as-required basis and intermittently every few days.

As hypnotics:
- use limited to 2–4 weeks at lower doses and intermittently;
- exclude other primary diagnosis (e.g. depression, substance misuse);
- consider newer alternatives (e.g. zopiclone and zolpidem).

Risk of dependence:
- withdrawal reactions are usually short-lived, lasting for up to a month;
- long-term dependence – treated by gradual withdrawal and psychological support with the addition of cognitive-behavioural therapy;
- long-term risks of using benzodiazepines need to be balanced against the benefits.

Beware of:

- benzodiazepines masking symptoms of depression;
- prescribed benzodiazepines being misused;
- benzodiazepines exacerbating disinhibition, especially those with personality disorders;
- accumulation of long-acting compounds which may impair skills and judgements (e.g. driving) – start with low doses initially;
- rebound phenomenon – withdrawal should be tapered slowly (e.g. over 2 weeks) to minimise rebound phenomenon even after short-term use.

$5HT_{1A}$ agonists (e.g. Buspirone)

- Anxiolytic effects take days or weeks to occur.
- Less side-effects compared to benzodiazepines.
- For short-term use only.
- Not effective for benzodiazepine-withdrawal symptoms.

Other hypnotics

Zaleplon, zolpidem, and zopiclone

- Although not benzodiazepines, they act on the same receptors as benzodiazepines.
- Short duration of action.

Chloral hydrate

- Properties similar to barbiturates.
- Previously used for children.
- Probably little effect in the elderly, though relatively safe.

Chlormethiazole

- Sedative and anticonvulsant properties.
- Rapid onset and short duration of action.
- Small risk of dependence.

Antihistamines

- Use usually unjustified.
- Long duration of action may cause day-time drowsiness.
- Sedative effects wear off after a few days.

Anti-epileptic drugs

Mechanisms of actions

Enhancement of GABA action	Benzodiazepines and phenobarbitone enhance activation of $GABA_A$ receptors. Vigabatrin inhibits the enzyme GABA-transaminase. Tigaine inhibits GABA uptake
Use-dependent inhibition of sodium channels, hence reducing nervous electrical excitability	Phenytoin, carbamazepine, valproate
Inhibition of T-type calcium channels	Ethosuximide

Withdrawal and switching of drugs

- Abrupt withdrawal may precipitate rebound seizures, especially for phenobaritone and benzodiazepine.
- When switching anticonvulsants, establish the second drug before withdrawing the first.

Phenytoin

Uses

- Effective against tonic–clonic and partial seizures.
- Narrow therapeutic window and non-linear dose–response relationship.
- Small changes in dosage may result in large changes in plasma concentrations. Hence plasma concentration monitoring essential.

Side-effects

- Coarse facies.
- Acne.
- Hirsuitism.
- Gingival hyperplasia.
- Vertigo, ataxia, headaches.
- Blood disorders: e.g. megaloblastic anaemia, leucopenia.

- Teratogenic effects (e.g. cleft palate in foetus).
- Severe idiosyncratic reactions: hepatitis and skin reactions (e.g. rashes, Stevens–Johnson syndrome).
- At toxic doses – blurred vision, confusion, drowsiness.

Interaction

- Interact with a large number of drugs via metabolism in the liver (e.g. warfarin).

Carbamazepine

Uses

- Indications:
  - simple and complex partial seizures;
  - tonic–clonic seizures secondary to a focal discharge.
- Wider therapeutic window than phenytoin, but plasma monitoring useful to determine optimal dose.

Side-effects
Overall incidence of side-effects lower than other anti-epileptics:

- Drowsiness, dizziness, ataxia.
- Gastrointestinal: nausea, vomiting, diarrhoea.
- Cardiovascular: arrhythmia and heart block.
- Blood disorders: e.g. aplastic anaemia, neutropenia.
- Skin disorders: e.g. rash, Stevens–Johnson syndrome.
- Liver problems: e.g. hepatitis.

Interactions

- Carbamazepine induces hepatic enzymes; hence, increases the metabolism of many other drugs (e.g. phenytoin, warfarin, etc.).
- Avoid combination of other anti-epileptics if possible.

Valproate

Actions and uses

- Mechanism of action uncertain – probably a combination of increasing GABA content in the brain and use-dependent inhibition of sodium channels.

- Used for most types of epilepsy (except absence seizures).
- Clinical effects poorly related to plasma levels – hence plasma monitoring unhelpful.
- Liver dysfunction and fatal hepatic failure occurs rarely. Hence important to monitor liver function before and during therapy.

Side-effects
Few overall side-effects compared to other anti-epileptics

- Impaired hepatic function and hepatotoxicity – rarely fatal.
- Transient hair loss (regrowth can be curly).
- Gastrointestinal: nausea and gastric irritation.
- Blood disorders: e.g. leukopenia.

Ethosuximide

Actions and uses

- Mechanism: inhibition of the T-channel calcium channel.
- Uses
  - simple absence seizures (mainly),
  - myoclonic seizures.

Side-effects

- Gastrointestinal: nausea, anorexia.
- Mood changes: depression, euphoria.
- Blood disorders: e.g. aplastic anaemia, leukopenia.

Benzodiazepines

- See section above.

Phenobarbitone

Action and uses

- Uses: effective against all forms of seizures, particularly tonic-clonic and partial seizures, but ineffective against absence seizures.
- Mechanism of action: enhanced GABA actions.
- Tolerance occurs – hence monitoring plasma level less helpful.
- Side-effects: sedation in adults and behavioural disturbances in children. Hence seldom used as first-line drug.

Side-effects

- Drowsiness, lethargy, depression.
- Paradoxical excitement, restlessness and confusion in the elderly.
- Behavioural disturbances and hyperkinesia in children.
- Megaloblastic anaemia (may be treated with folic acid).

Interactions

- Induces microsomal enzymes. Hence interacts with many drugs (including other anticonvulsants and warfarin).

Withdrawal

- Rebound withdrawal is especially common.

Vigabatrin

Actions and uses

- Designed as specific inhibitor of GABA-transaminase (which metabolises GABA).
- Hence increases GABA in the brain.
- Uses: treatment of partial epilepsy with or without secondary generalisation, restricted to patients in whom all other treatments are ineffective (due to its side-effects of visual field defects).

Side-effects

- Drowsiness.
- Visual field defects.
- Irritability and agitation.
- Visual disturbance (e.g. diplopia); and retinal disorders (e.g. peripheral retinal atrophy).

Antimuscarinic agents

- Uses:
  - to counteract the Parkinsonian side-effects of antipsychotic drugs;
  - to counteract acute severe dystonic reactions associated with antipsychotic drugs.
- Mechanism of action: antagonist at muscarinic receptors, thus correcting the relative central cholinergic excess which occurs in Parkinsonism.

- For Parkinsonian symptoms: oral orphenadrine and trihexyphenidyl (benzhexol); benzatropine and procyclidine.
- For acute dystonic reaction: IM or IV procyclidine or benzatropine.
- Side-effects: dry mouth, blurred vision, gastrointestinal disturbances, confusion.

Neurochemical effects of ECT

Mechanisms of actions of ECT are controversial. A recent literature review* showed the following results.

- ECT alters several 5-HT receptor subtypes in the CNS:
  - 5-HT$_{1A}$ post-synaptic receptors are sensitised, but those in the pre-synaptic neurones are not;
  - 5-HT$_3$ receptors in hippocampus are sensitised, leading to an increase in the release of neurotransmitters such as glutamate and GABA;
  - auto-receptor functions are decreased in NA in locus coeruleus and DA neurones in substantia nigra, causing in a release in NA and DA.

Adverse drug reactions (ADRs)

Dose-related vs idiosyncratic adverse drug reactions

Dose-related ADR	Idiosyncratic ADR
Common	Relatively rare
A range of severity	Usually harmful, sometimes fatal
Reactions are much more likely in those taking high doses	Reactions may occur with low doses
Most patients, taking sufficiently large doses, may experience reactions	Only a few susceptible patients will experience reactions
Unrelated to genetic factors	Usually associated with genetic factors (e.g. specific enzyme deficiency)

*Ishihara K, Sasa M. Japanese Journal of Pharmacology, 1999, 80(3): 185–9.

Examples: Parkinsonian symptoms with antipsychotic drugs; drowsiness with diazepam	Examples: fatal hepatic failure with valproate; prolonged recovery from anaesthetics in individuals with plasma cholinesterase variants; neuroleptic malignant syndrome with antipsychotics

Information database for adverse drug reactions and reporting them

- Any drugs may produce unanticipated adverse reactions.
- A central database to record, monitor, analyse and act on these reactions is important for patient's safety.
- The Committee on Safety of Medicine (CSM) of the Medicines Control Agency takes on this role after the thalidomide tragedy in 1964.
- All doctors, dentists, pharmacists and coroners should report any unwanted or unexpected adverse reactions.
- For 'black triangle drugs' (i.e. drugs under intense surveillance), all adverse reactions should be reported.
- For established drugs, only serious adverse drug reactions should be reported.
- Reports can be made to: Medicines Control Agency, CSM Freepost, London SW8 5BR, UK. (0800 731 6789).
- Prepaid 'Yellow cards' for spontaneous reporting are available inside the back cover of every British National Formulary (BNF).
- Regional centres also collect data.
- The post-licensing division of the MCA ensure that medicines meet acceptable standards of safety and efficacy.
- Reporting may protect patients because it
  - provides 'early warnings' of previously unsuspected adverse drug reactions;
  - can be used to elicit factors that predispose to particular ADRs;
  - can compare ADR profiles between medicines within therapeutic classes;
  - permits continued safety monitoring throughout the duration of a product's use as a marketed medicine.

Prescription of controlled drugs

General

- Controlled drugs are defined and regulated under The Misuse of Drugs Act 1971.
- The penalties applied to offences involving the manufacture, supply and possession of controlled drugs are graded depending on the harmfulness of a drug if it is misused.
- There are 3 classes of controlled drugs. The following lists are selective and not complete.

  Class A – cocaine, diamorphine (heroin), lysergide (LSD), methadone, ectasy, morphine, pethidine or opium, phencyclidine, Class B substances prepared for injection.

  Class B – amphetamines, barbiturates, cannabis, cannabis resin, codeine.

  Class C – drugs related to amphetamines; most benzodiazepines; androgenic and anabolic steroids.

The Misuse of Drugs Regulations 1985:

- defined the classes of persons who are authorised to supply and possess controlled drugs while acting in their professional capacities;
- lay down the conditions under which these activities may be carried out.
- prescribed 5 schedules specifying the requirements governing issue of prescriptions and record keeping:

  Schedule 1
  - possession and supply of substances not used medicinally prohibited except with Home Office authority;
  - includes cannabis and LSD etc.

  Schedule 2
  - subjected to full controlled drug requirements relating to prescriptions and safe custody, and the need to keep registers;
  - includes diamorphine, morphine, pethidine, amphetamine etc.

  Schedule 3
  - subjected to special prescription requirements, but not to safety custody requirements nor the need to keep registers;
  - includes barbiturates, temazepam, buprenorphine, etc.

  Schedules 4 and 5
  - not subjected to drug prescription or safe custody requirements.

Prescription requirements

- *Signed* and *dated* (*not* computer generated) by the prescriber, with the prescriber's address.
- Stated in the prescriber's own handwriting in ink or otherwise so as to be indelible.
  1. The name and address of the patient.
  2. The preparation, the form (e.g. tablets) and, where appropriate, the strength of the preparation.
  3. The total quantity of the preparation, or the number of dose units, *in both words and figures*.
  4. The dose may be ordered to be dispensed by instalments (a total of 14 days' treatment by instalment of any drug listed in Schedule 2), but the amount of the instalments and the intervals to be observed must be specified.
- 'Repeats' not to be ordered on the same form.
- Validity of prescription only for 13 weeks from the date stated thereon.

Notification of drug misusers

- From May 1997, doctors are no longer required to send to the Home Office particulars of drug addicts.
- However, doctors are expected to report on a standard form cases of drug misuse to their local Drug Misuse Database (DMD).
- Notification to the Drug Misuse Database should be made when a patient first presents with a drug problem or re-presents after a gap of 6 months or more.
- All types of problem-drug misuse should be reported including opioid, benzodiazepine, and CNS stimulant.

5 Preparation for clinical part of MRCPsych Part 1 examination

Clinical skills

History taking

In the history it is important to elicit the factual information necessary to define the patient's problems, suggest diagnostic possibilities and the factors which may have initiated and maintained the patient's illness. The areas to be covered include:

Background information
- Name, age, occupation, marital status, housing situation.
- Source of referral.

Presenting complaint
- Reasons for referral.
- Description of symptom onset, duration and progression.
- Follow-up each presenting symptom.
- Cluster together questions about particular clinical syndromes.
- Relationship of symptoms to any problems in the patient's life.
- Effect that the illness has had on the patient's life.

Past psychiatric history
- Main symptoms and diagnosis of previous illnesses.
- Previous acts of deliberate self-harm/suicidal intent.
- Treatments received (including ECT) and their effects.
- Hospital admissions.
- Detention under the Mental Health Act.

Past medical history
- Serious physical illnesses, operations or accidents.
- Current physical health.
- Current medication.

Family history
- Depiction of family tree (may be helpful).
- Details on parents and siblings.
- Age, health, occupation, personality and relationship with patient.
- History of psychiatric or physical illnesses in the family.

Personal history
- Birth details.
- Early development including milestones.
- Separations or traumas.
- Childhood health and temperament.
- Neurotic symptoms, e.g. temper tantrums, bed-wetting.
- Schools, intellectual ability, relationships with peers and teachers.
- Higher education.
- Occupational history.
- Relationship/marital history.
- Sexual history – may not be appropriate to include a detailed sexual history in an initial diagnostic interview unless sexual dysfunction is a presenting problem.
- Children.
- Current social situation including housing arrangements.

Drug and alcohol history
- Cigarettes, alcohol and illicit drugs.
- Amount, circumstances of use, physical effects.
- Symptoms of withdrawal or dependence.
- Associated problems – work, relationships, financial, social, criminal.

Forensic history
- Any trouble with the police.
- Arrests, convictions, type of offences, periods of imprisonment.

Premorbid personality
- How would the patient describe himself.
- Relationships with others – ease of making and sustaining friendships.
- Interests and hobbies.
- Predominant mood.
- Attitudes to work and responsibility.
- Standards and morals.
- Habits.

Mental state examination

The mental state examination involves a description of the symptoms and behaviour that are present at the time of the interview. Some of the information would already have been gathered during the history but other areas will need to be covered:

Appearance and behaviour

- Clothing.
- Cleanliness/self-care.
- Body build.
- Facial expression.
- Gait.
- Posture.
- Motor activity.
- Rapport.
- Social manner.

Speech

- Rate.
- Quantity.
- Flow.
- Content.

Mood

- Quality.
- Variations.
- Congruity.

Thoughts

- Delusions.
- Ideas of reference.
- Passivity phenomena.
- Depersonalisation.
- Preoccupations, ruminations, obsessions.
- Suicidal ideation.

Perception

- Illusions.
- Hallucinations.

Cognitive functioning

- The *Mini Mental State Examination* covers different aspects of cognitive function and can be performed quite quickly. See table given below.
- Tests of frontal lobe function include:
  Verbal fluency – words beginning with F, A or S in 1 min (> 30 = normal).
  Abstracting ability – interpretation of proverbs.
  Luria's motor tests – making fist, slicing air and slapping movement with hand repeated in sequence.

Insight

The extent of the patient's understanding of his illness.

- Does the patient think that he is ill?
- How does he explain his symptoms?
- Does he think that treatment is necessary? What type?

Physical examination

Examiners expect the candidate to have conducted a physical examination. There may not be sufficient time for a thorough physical but the pulse and blood pressure could be checked along with signs that could support the suspected diagnosis:

- Signs of Parkinsonism – facies, festinant gait, tremor, rigidity.
- Thyroid signs.
- Autonomic over-arousal.
- Previous deliberate self-harm scars.
- Signs of alcoholic liver disease or IV drug abuse.
- Neurological examination.

Mini mental state examination (Folstein et al.)

Action	Questions		Points
Orientation	Year	Country	One point each
	Season	County	Total: 5 + 5
	Month	Town/city	

	Date Name/type of building	
	Day Floor of building	

Registration	Ask the patient to repeat three words that you will say, e.g. apple, table, penny Repeat until all three are remembered	One point for each word Total: 3
Attention and calculation	From 100, keep subtracting 7 and say each answer; stop after 5 responses *OR*, spell the word 'world' backwards	Total: 5
Recall	Ask the patient to recall the three words given earlier	Total: 3
Naming	Ask the patient to name two objects that you will show, e.g. watch, pen	Total: 2
Repeating	Ask patient to repeat: 'no ifs, and or buts'	Total: 1
Reading	Write 'close your eyes' on a piece of paper, and ask the patient to read the words and to do what it says	Total: 1
Writing	Ask the patient to write a short sentence	Total: 1
Three-stage command	Present the patient with a piece of paper, ask him to take it in his left hand, fold it in half and place it on the floor	Total: 3
Construction	Ask the patient to copy this drawing of two interlocking pentagons:	Total: 1

Total score (out of 30 points):

Consequences of brain lesions

Frontal lobes:

- Pseudodepression – loss of drive (abulia), apathy, hypokinesis.
- Pseudopsychopathy – restless, impulsive, facetious, antisocial behaviour.

- Expressive language disorders – Brocas area.
- Spastic paralysis – primary motor cortex.
- Urinary incontinence.

Temporal lobes:

- Short-term memory deficits, amnesic syndrome.
- Receptive language disorders.
- Visual field defects; auditory perceptual deficits.

Parietal lobes:

- Spatial disorientation, impaired location and topographical memory.
- Tactile agnosias; apraxias.
- Dyslexia, dyscalculia.
- Contralateral visual field defect.

Occipital lobes:

- Cortical blindness.
- Visual agnosias.
- Pure word blindness.
- Complex visual hallucinations.

Formulation

Formulation is a way of communicating the information obtained from the history and mental state examination in a clear and concise manner. It should include:

- a brief demographic description of the patient;
- description of the main problems;
- a summary of the positive and important negative findings;
- discussion of differential diagnoses with reasons for and against each suggestion;
- aetiological factors:
  - predisposing,
  - precipitating,
  - perpetuating.

Psychodynamic formulation

The examiners expect the candidate to gather information relevant to a psychodynamic formulation. This information should be available from the history. The following should be taken into consideration:

1. *Current life situation* – describe current symptoms in terms of feeling states and relationships with spouses, work or with parents in the present. Consider primary or secondary gains of the symptoms.
2. *Infantile object relations* – family relationships in childhood which could have contributed to the illness.
3. *Relationship with interviewer* – evidence of transference and counter-transference.
4. Evidence of defence mechanisms used and the avoidance of particular subjects.

Long case – exam before Spring 2003

Structure and format

The Part I exam consists of an MCQ paper and a clinical examination. The clinical exam involves an interview with a patient for 1 hour followed by 30 min with the examiners. The time with the examiners is divided into three sections:

1. Presentation of the case.
2. Interview of patient.
3. Discussion of the case.

The clinical case is the most important part, because a candidate must pass this in order to pass the exam overall. It is also an extremely stressful event but it can be made less so by good preparation and good clinical skills.

Practice exams are useful:

- Practise with different examiners – practising with two mock examiners who are College examiners adds realism.
- Practise with different types of cases which are likely to appear in the exam.
- Practise interviewing the patient in front of the mock examiners.

Practical points

- Allow plenty of time before the exam or stay in a nice hotel the night before – travelling is stressful.

- Arrive a bit early.
- Dress smartly and look professional.

Difficult patients

- Remember that it is often difficult for examination centres to find a large number of suitable patients for the exam.
- The examiners will know from the case summaries whether the patient has a complicated history or is a difficult historian.
- Do not panic, try to collect as much information as you can.
- Problems may arise due to the psychopathology of the patient or a failure of technique/empathy on the part of the interviewer.
- If a patient is talking very little, try to:
  - ask open questions about topics the patient is prepared to discuss;
  - use empathic sounds and ask for elaboration of answers.
- If a patient is talking too much about irrelevancies or going off at a tangent, try to:
  - avoid empathic gestures;
  - ask the patient to return to the topic;
  - use more closed questions.

Interview with patient

- Before the patient enters it is helpful to write down a list of headings for the history, especially those areas that you might forget to ask about.
- Introduce yourself to the patient, explain what will happen during the interview.
- Explain about the time and apologise in advance for interruptions.
- When taking the history,
  - write on one side of the paper,
  - clearly order notes,
  - you are allowed to ask about diagnosis.
- Conduct a physical examination.
- Aim to finish early but ask the patient to remain in the room.
- Check notes for missing information.
- Explain about the interview in front of the examiners and thank the patient.

Thinking time

- It is helpful to write out the first couple of lines of the presentation and rehearse it so that the first impression you give the examiners will be positive.
- Consider differential diagnoses and your reasons for and against each.
- Do not forget co-morbidity.
- Consider aetiological factors relevant to this case.
- Think about what questions you may be asked.

The examiners

A College observer, who does not take part in the exam itself, may be present.

- Remain calm and confident – you have presented many cases before.
- Remember that the first few minutes are the most important.
- Make eye contact with both examiners when presenting.
- Speak clearly.
- Present the case in a logical way and mention the physical examination findings.
- Interview of patient:
  - note the questions before calling the patient;
  - introduce the patient to examiners and explain that it is you who are being tested;
  - cover both question areas;
  - avoid very leading questions;
  - thank the patient at the end and escort him/her out of the room.
- During the discussion:
  - Do not argue with the examiners.
  - Do not lie.
  - Try not to dig yourself into a hole by mentioning something silly or something that you know nothing about.

After the exam

- You may not have a clue as to how the exam went, or you may be convinced of failure but in reality may have performed well enough to pass.
- Forget about it.
- Enjoy the time between the exam and the day of the results.

Dealing with failure

- Remember that a lot of good candidates fail the exam.
- The overall pass rate is usually less than 50%.
- Request feedback – this will give you an overall mark out of 10, comments on performance in each section and advice on improving performance.
- Reapply.

OSCE (exam in or after Spring 2003)

The College is planning to replace the clinical long case in the Part I exam with an Observed Structured Clinical Examination (OSCE) which would assess a range of essential clinical competencies using a number of different scenarios in a well-standardised format. There will be a minimum of 12 stations comprising of clinical scenarios including vignettes, simulated patients and video material. This proposed change is aimed to be introduced into the Part I examination in Spring 2003.

Further details are not available from the College at the time of writing. OSCE has been used for a few years in the UK for undergraduate assessments, followed recently by a few postgraduate examinations such as the DRCOG. The following notes are written based on these experiences adapted to the MRCPsych Part 1 examination. However, candidates must ascertain the current regulations from the College.

Format

Candidates rotate amongst at least 12 'stations' and spend a fixed length of time (usually 5–10 min) at each station. Usually, a bell signals that the time allotted to a station is up and for all candidates to move on to the next station. At each station, there is an examiner and written instructions for the candidates to carry out a task. Occasionally, the examiner gives standard instructions to the candidates to carry out a task. The examiner assesses the candidate's performance against a tight marking scheme prepared in advance by the College. The marking scheme usually specifies precisely the types of responses from or behaviour of the candidates for which to award scores. The candidate's mark is an aggregate of the individual scores at all the 'stations'. In this way, all candidates will be asked to perform the same tasks and assessed in the same way.

Assessment criteria

It is likely that the assessment criteria will be based on a combination of:

• Knowledge.
• Clinical skills – e.g. history taking, mental state examination, interpretation of investigation results.
• Communication skills.
• Attitudes.

Probable tasks

Tasks in the OSCE may include:

1. *Taking specific aspects of history* from a real or simulated patient.
2. *Assessing mental state* – assessing specific aspects of mental state (probably from a video extract) and presenting the findings to the examiner.
3. *Communication* (usually a simulated patient or role play with the examiner) – e.g. breaking bad news (e.g. the diagnosis of dementia or schizophrenia to a relative), obtaining informed consent (e.g. for ECT).
4. *Physical examination* – e.g. simple neurological examination, taking blood pressure.
5. *Interpreting investigative results* – e.g. lithium level.

Items (1)–(3) will probably be the most important. Future examinations may include cardiopulmonary resuscitation (check syllabus).

General advice

• Read (or listen to) the instructions carefully, and perform only the tasks asked for. No marks will be given to other tasks.
• Pay attention to all 3 areas: knowledge; skills; communication and attitude. Although the proportion of marks allocated to these 3 areas varies at each station, it is likely that marks will be allocated to all 3 aspects in every task.

- Move on at a reasonable pace. Since marks are allocated for aspects of every task, you will certainly lose marks heavily if you do not complete all the tasks. Take hints from the examiners to move on.
- Thank the patient/simulated patient/examiner at the end of every station.
- Concentrate on the task in hand: forget what went on in the previous stations.

Specific advice

Taking history – The skills necessary here are exactly the same as those for history taking in the long case (see above), except that you need to focus on one aspect of the history although you know nothing about the patient beforehand.

Mental state examination – Again, the skills necessary are the same as those in the clinical long case (see above). However, unlike the clinical case above, you will see the patient for the first time, and you may be asked to assess a patient on video. You will be asked specifically to focus on one or two areas (e.g. thoughts, perceptions), and you will need to organise and present the findings immediately. It is even more important to be structured in assessing and presenting mental state examination findings.

Communicating bad news

- find out what the patient or relative already knows or senses;
- find out how much the patient or relative is ready to know at the time;
- explain diagnosis, treatment and prognosis slowly and in simple language;
- give details about expected effects of treatment, social and practical support available (or people they can see for such support);
- provide opportunities for patients to ask questions, express their fears, or raise other issues.

6 | Specific clinical disorders

Delirium and dementia

Delirium

Epidemiology

- Occurs in up to 15% of patients in general hospitals.
- More common with:
  - increasing age,
  - brain damage/dementia,
  - anxiety,
  - sensory under- or over-stimulation,
  - physical illnesses.

Classification

See chapter on psychopathology.

Clinical features

- Rapid onset, fluctuating course, particularly worse at night.
- Possible agitation or retardation with reduced speech.
- Anxiety; fright; perplexity.
- Muddled thoughts; ideas of reference or delusions.
- Illusions; hallucinations, particularly visual.
- Disorientation in time and place; memory impairment; poor insight.

Aetiology

- Infection.
- Cerebrovascular disease; cardiovascular disease.
- Drug intoxication or drug withdrawal.
- Hypoglycaemia; hypoxia; metabolic failures.
- Head injury; epilepsy.

Dementia

Features

- Dementia is a global decline in functioning affecting
  - memory,
  - intellect,
  - personality.
- Usually chronic or progressive.
- Most causes are irreversible but a small number may be treated.
- Prevalence of dementia increases with age: 5% of people aged over 65 and up to 20% of people aged over 80.

Some causes of dementia

- *Degenerative:*
  - Alzheimer's disease.
  - Lewy body dementia.
  - Pick's disease.
  - Huntington's chorea.
  - Parkinson's disease.
  - Multiple sclerosis.
- *Vascular:*
  - Multi-infarct dementia.
  - Subarachnoid.
  - Subdural haematoma.
- *Tumours:*
  - Primary and secondary tumours.
- *Infection:*
  - Neurosyphilis.
  - Encephalitis.
  - Creutzfeld-Jakob disease.
  - AIDS.
- *Metabolic:*
  - Liver or kidney failure.
  - Hypothyroidism.
  - Porphyria.
  - Deficiencies of vitamin B12, folic acid, thiamine.
- *Alcohol*
- *Trauma and anoxia*

Investigations

- Assessment within the home and by different disciplines, e.g. OT, SW.
- History from informants.
- Blood tests – FBC, ESR, U&E, LFT, TFT, Glucose, B12, folate, syphilis serology.
- Urine sample, ECG, chest X-ray.
- More specialised tests:
  EEG – may be normal, show non-specific changes or diffuse slow activity.
  CT/MRI – cortical atrophy, ventricular enlargement, infarcts.
  SPECT/PET – e.g. deficits in parietotemporal areas in Alzheimer's.
- Psychological assessment.

Classification (ICD10)

General criteria for diagnosing dementia:

1. Symptoms present for at least 6 months.
2. No clouding of consciousness.
3. Deterioration in memory (grade depending on stage of illness – mild/ moderate/severe).
4. Deterioration in other cognitive functions – judgement, thinking, planning, organising, information processing.
5. Change in emotional control, motivation or social behaviour, with at least one of the following:
   - Emotional lability.
   - Irritability.
   - Apathy.
   - Coarsening of social behaviour.

Alzheimer's disease

Clinical features

Mild
- Appearance and behaviour – fatigue, occasional odd behaviours, more pronounced personality traits, loss of interest.
- Speech – some word-finding difficulties.
- Mood – anxiety, depression.
- Memory – initially minor forgetfulness which may be difficult to distinguish from that caused by normal ageing, difficulties with new learning, impaired concentration.

- Able to live independently but experience problems with complicated tasks.

Moderate

- Appearance and behaviour – neglect of personal care, decline of social behaviour, restricted activities, motor restlessness or inactivity; may become aggressive, wake up at night, wandering.
- Speech – narrowed vocabulary, may ask repeated questions, dysphasia, dysarthria.
- Mood – irritability, emotional lability, catastrophic reactions when faced with limitations.
- Possible misidentification, hallucinations and delusions.
- Memory – deteriorates further with only very familiar material remembered; subjects forget names of familiar people; forget local geography; forget what they have been doing from day to day.
- Disorientated in time and space; less able to read and write; apraxias and agnosias.
- Need help with daily living and can perform only basic household tasks. Ability to live independently is seriously affected.

Severe

- Severe personality deterioration.
- No communication.
- Intellectual functioning severely impaired – unable to recognise family members; unable to retain information; absence of intelligible ideation.
- Physical signs – increased muscle tone, primitive reflexes, incontinence.
- Need assistance with all daily tasks.
- Physical state deteriorates to death.

Aetiology

Age:
- Incidence rates increase rapidly with advancing age.
- More common in females (even after adjusting for life expectancy).

Genetic:

Familial studies – first degree relatives have three times the risk of developing dementia; some rare pedigrees show autosomal dominant inheritance.

Chromosome 21 – location of amyloid precursor protein gene, link discovered because of increased rate of dementia in people with Down's syndrome (trisomy 21).

Chromosome 19 – location of the E4 allele of apolipoprotein E; homozygotes of this allele have an increased risk of developing dementia, Apo E may promote the deposition of amyloid.

Chromosome 14 – identified as a site of genetic linkage for presenile dementia.

Environmental:

- Head injuries may predispose to dementia.
- Aluminium – may increase production of amyloid peptide.

Neurotransmitters:

Choline – the cholinergic system is associated with memory functioning. Low cholinergic activity is found in Alzheimer's patients and the decline in choline acetyltransferase correlates with the decline in cognitive function.

Noradrenaline and serotonin – evidence of cell loss, may be involved in producing other symptoms of dementia such as aggression and mood disorder.

Somatostatin – reduced levels.

Neuropathology:

- Macroscopic:
  - Brain atrophy, sulcal widening, ventricular enlargement.
- Microscopic:
  - Plaques – contain amyloid; severity of illness correlates with the number of plaques;
  - Neurofibrillary tangles – paired helical filaments of Tau protein and ubiquitin;
  - Amyloid protein deposits in blood vessels;
  - Lewy bodies, Hirano bodies, astrocytes and granulovacuolar degeneration.

Multi-infarct dementia

Clinical features

- Fairly sudden onset, stepwise progression with features that reflect the areas of damaged cortex.
- Personality relatively preserved.
- May be unsteady on feet or may fall.
- Affective symptoms common – depression, anxiety, lability.
- Confusion may occur at night.
- Focal cognitive deficits.

- Insight maintained until late stages.
- Physical signs – hypertension and other signs of atherosclerosis; TIA's; neurological signs, e.g., brisk reflexes, pseudobulbar palsy, sensory deficits.

Aetiology

- Infarction of brain tissue.
- Risk factors – increasing age, hypertension, smoking, high cholesterol, alcohol, cardiovascular disease.

Lewy body dementia

Clinical features

- Spontaneous features of Parkinsonism – tremor, rigidity, postural change, bradykinesia, gait disturbance.
- Fluctuating impairment affecting memory and higher functions.
- Deficits in attention, visuospatial ability and frontal subcortical skills.
- Visual hallucinations – usually detailed and recurring.
- Hallucinations of other types; systematised delusions.
- Repeated falls.
- Sensitivity to neuroleptics.

Aetiology

- Large number of Lewy bodies particularly in subcortical areas.
- Reduced amounts of choline acetyl transferase and dopamine.

Subcortical dementia

Subcortical dementia can occur with

- Huntington's disease,
- Parkinson's disease,
- Progressive supranuclear palsy,
- Hydrocephalus,
- AIDS dementia complex,
- Subcortical infarctions, infections and tumours.

Clinical features

- Apathy, irritability.
- Affective disturbance is common – particularly depression.
- Dysarthria.

- Reduced cognition and motor ability.
- Intellectual deterioration, memory loss.

Addictions

ICD10 classification of disorders associated with the use and abuse of alcohol and other psychoactive substances

First, specification of the substance. Mental and behavioural disorders due to use of:
Alcohol,
Opioids,
Cannabinoids,
Sedatives or hypnotics,
Cocaine,
Other stimulants, including caffeine,
Hallucinogens,
Tobacco,
Volatile solvents,
Multiple drug use and use of other psychoactive substances.
Then, *specification of the clinical condition:*
Acute intoxication,
Harmful use,
Dependence syndrome,
Withdrawal state,
Withdrawal state with delirium,
Psychotic disorder,
Amnesic syndrome,
Residual and late-onset psychotic disorder,
Other mental and behavioural disorders,
Unspecified mental and behavioural disorders.

Classification of a dependence syndrome (ICD10): 3 or more of the following symptoms occurring within 1 year:
Strong desire/compulsion to use substance,
Impaired ability to control substance use,

Withdrawal state,
Tolerance,
Neglect of alternative pleasures/interests,
Persist with use despite evidence of harm.

Alcohol

Definitions

Excess consumption – weekly intake exceeding 21 units for females and 28 units for males (DOH guidelines).
Harmful use – pattern of alcohol consumption that causes damage to health, either mental or physical.
Problem drinking – drinking that has caused an alcohol-related problem; person may or may not be dependent on alcohol.
Dependence – a psychophysiological state caused by repeated use of alcohol.

Epidemiology

- Lifetime prevalence of alcoholism approx. 14%.
- More common in:
  - men (M:F = 4:1);
  - urban areas;
  - homeless people;
  - divorced/separated people;
  - certain occupations – publicans, chefs, executives, actors, doctors.

Complications

Gastrointestinal – carcinoma of mouth/pharynx/oesophagus; oesophageal varices; gastritis; peptic ulcer; pancreatitis; fatty liver; hepatitis; cirrhosis; hepatic carcinoma.
Cardiovascular – hypertension; cardiomyopathy; CVA; anaemia.
Neurological – peripheral neuropathy; cerebellar degeneration; head injury; epilepsy.
Other physical – hypoglycaemia; vitamin deficiencies; foetal alcohol syndrome; pneumonia; TB; myopathy.
Social – domestic violence; divorce; unemployment; accidents; crime.

Psychiatric – Wernicke's encephalopathy; Korsakoff's psychosis; mood disorder; suicide; personality change; psychosexual problems; pathological jealousy; alcoholic hallucinosis; alcoholic dementia.

Investigations

- Describe a drinking day, drinking diary.
- CAGE questions (2+ indicates abuse):
  Have you thought you should **C**ut down on your drinking?
  Have people **A**nnoyed you by criticising your drinking?
  Have you felt **G**uilty about drinking?
  Do you have an **E**ye-opener in the morning to steady your nerves?
- Breathalyzer test
- *Blood tests* – full range; look particularly for raised MCV and abnormal LFT's.

Alcohol related syndromes

Alcohol dependence

Clinical features (Edwards and Gross)

- Narrowing of repertoire – stereotyped pattern of drinking.
- Salience – alcohol takes precedence over everything; less time spent doing other things.
- Increased tolerance – takes increasingly more alcohol to get the same effects.
- Repeated withdrawal symptoms – see features listed below.
- Relief or avoidance of withdrawal symptoms by further drinking.
- Subjective compulsion to drink.
- Reinstatement after abstinence.

Classification (ICD10)
See above.

Aetiology

Genetics
- Family studies – increased incidence in families of alcohol dependent people.
- Twin studies – greater concordance for monozygotic twins.
- Adoption studies – 4 times increased incidence in adopted sons of alcohol dependent biological parents.

Biological

- Sensitivity to the acute intoxicating effects may be reduced so that more alcohol is consumed to achieve the effect and the risk of tolerance is increased.
- Alcohol may cause the release of dopamine which acts as a reinforcer to the drinking.

Psychosocial

- Association with psychiatric illnesses perhaps as a way of self-medication; e.g. depression, anxiety, social phobias.
- Association with dissocial personality disorder.
- Societal factors – availability, cost, licensing, customs and beliefs.

Learning

- Observational learning – children may copy the drinking habits of their parents.
- Expected positive effects – increases the degree of subsequent use.
- Withdrawal avoidance – the use of alcohol to stop unpleasant withdrawal symptoms helps to reinforce continued drinking.

Alcohol withdrawal states

Clinical features

- Typically occur on waking when the blood alcohol level has dropped.
- Agitated; startled easily; tremor.
- Nausea; retching; sweating; muscle cramps.
- Mood disturbance; insomnia.
- Distorted perception; hallucinations.
- Convulsions.
- *Delirium tremens:*
  - Begins 1–4 days after abstinence.
  - Important because of mortality rate of 5%.
  - Anxiety; fear; tremor; restlessness; insomnia.
  - Fluctuations in consciousness; disorientation.
  - Hallucinations:
    Often visual, may be Lilliputian.
    Auditory and tactile hallucinations can also occur.
  - Autonomic changes: fever, pyrexia, tachycardia, hypertension, pupil dilatation.
  - Electrolyte disturbance; leucocytosis; abnormal LFTs.
  - Convulsions.

Wernicke's encephalopathy

Clinical features

- Clouding of consciousness and confusion.
- Nystagmus; opthalmoplegia.
- Ataxia.
- Peripheral neuropathy.

Aetiology

- Severe thiamine deficiency; e.g., due to excessive vomiting and bowel diseases causing malabsorption.

Complications

- Can progress to Korsakoff's psychosis if untreated.

Korsakoff's psychosis

Clinical features

- 'Amnesic syndrome':
  - Immediate recall usually preserved.
  - Impaired learning of new information.
  - Recent memory more disturbed than remote memory.
  - Disorientation in time.
  - Relative preservation of other cognitive functions.
- No clouding of consciousness.
- Confabulation may occur.
- Peripheral neuropathy.

Alcoholic hallucinosis

Clinical features

- Rare.
- Patient distressed and restless.
- Organised auditory hallucinations, often threats and critical remarks.
- Occur in clear consciousness.

Alcoholic dementia

Clinical features

- Greater risk in women.
- Mild to moderate cognitive impairment which improves with abstinence.
- Atrophy can be seen on CT/MRI scans.
- Other physical signs of alcoholism.

Illicit drugs

See the section on pharmacology for information on:

- Classes of controlled drugs.
- Misuse of Drugs Regulations.
- Schedules of prescribing drugs.
- Notification.

Epidemiology, criteria and aetiology

Epidemiology

- Prevalence of use is difficult to obtain due to its illicit nature.
- More common in:
  - younger age group – teens and early twenties;
  - unemployed;
  - deprived areas of large cities.
- Patterns of use:
  - experimental,
  - recreational,
  - compulsive.

Criteria for dependence
See under classification for alcohol dependence

Aetiology of drug abuse

Environmental factors:
- Access, availability and selling pressures of the drug.
- Peer pressure.
- Social deprivation.
- Family factors which influence drug use:
  - positive family history of drug use;

– poor relationships within the family;
– unconventional social attitudes.

Personal factors:
- Personality – impulsiveness, sensation seeking, aggression, dissocial behaviour.
- Deviant behaviour in childhood is a predictor of drug use in early adult life.

Psychological factors:
- modelling;
- positive reinforcement due to positive experiences when using the drug;
- repeated use to avoid unpleasant withdrawal symptoms;
- psychoanalytic – fixation at oral stage of development.

Cannabis

- Most widely used illicit drug in the UK.
- Active ingredient delta 9 tetrahydrocannabinol.
- Acts on G protein receptor.
- *Effects:*
  – depend on circumstances of use, expectations and previous experience;
  – relaxation, euphoria;
  – temporal distortion, greater sensory awareness, impaired judgement, suspiciousness;
  – tachycardia, hypertension, dry mouth, constipation, ataxia, nystagmus.
- *Withdrawal:*
  – restlessness, irritability, insomnia, anorexia, nausea.
- *Harmful effects:*
  – aggression, anxiety, panic attacks;
  – personality change;
  – flashbacks, depersonalisation/derealisation;
  – cognitive impairment.

Stimulants

Cocaine

- Blocks reuptake of dopamine.
- *Effects:*

- last about 20 min;
- euphoria, excess energy, excitement, agitation, lack of hunger;
- dilated pupils, sweating, tremor, tachycardia, hypertension, nausea/vomiting;
- impaired functioning, judgement affected;
- may develop a toxic psychosis – paranoia, persecutory delusions, ideas of reference, hallucinations;
- formication – 'cocaine bug'.
- *Withdrawal:*
  - 'crash', fatigue, dysphoria, anxiety, irritability, depression, insomnia, intense craving.
- *Harmful effects:*
  - hyperthermia, convulsions, death;
  - heart attack, heart failure, stroke;
  - perforation of nasal septum.

Amphetamine

- Action, effects and withdrawal effects are very similar to those produced by cocaine.
- Release and block reuptake of serotonin and dopamine.
- May develop tolerance.
- May develop a toxic psychosis which can resemble schizophrenia.

Opioids

- Examples: heroin, buprenorphine (temgesic), morphine, methadone, dihydrocodiene.
- Stimulate opioid receptors.
- *Effects:*
  - euphoria, drowsiness;
  - analgesia, anorexia, reduced libido;
  - bradycardia, hypotension, constipation, miosis, respiratory depression.
- *Withdrawal:*
  - occurs within 4–12 hours of last use of heroin;
  - peaks at 48 hours and ends after a week;
  - sweating, shivering, 'goose bumps', uncontrollable yawning, rhinnorhoea, excess lacrimation;
  - dilated pupils, aching limbs, nausea, diarrhoea, abdominal cramps;
  - fatigue, dysphoria, insomnia, craving.

- *Harmful effects:*
  - overdose;
  - IV use – HIV infection, hepatitis, skin abscess, SBE, DVT;
  - social – accidents, crime, family breakdown.

Hallucinogens

LSD

- Serotonin agonist.
- *Effects:*
  - heightened and distorted perception, synaesthesia, intense emotions;
  - altered sense of time and place;
  - hallucinations and delusions may sometimes occur.
- *Withdrawal* – no effects.
- *Harmful effects:*
  - flashbacks – recurrence of all or part of the original experience, may be associated with depression or anxiety;
  - acute psychosis;
  - accidents.

MDMA (ecstasy)

- Hallucinogenic amphetamine.
- Stimulates serotonin release and blocks reuptake.
- *Effects:*
  - stimulatory effects like that of amphetamine;
  - hallucinogenic effects like that of LSD; increased perceptual awareness;
  - elevated mood/euphoria, feeling of being close to others;
  - sweating, tachycardia, anorexia, bruxism.
- *Harmful effects:*
  - hyperthermia, hypertensive crisis, spontaneous intracranial haemorrhage;
  - death from cardiac arrhythmias, recurrent jaundice, convulsions, neurotoxicity.

Solvents

- CNS depressants.
- May increase fluidity of nerve cell membranes and affect GABA function.

- *Effects:*
  - initial euphoria, disinhibition, disorganised behaviour, confusion;
  - dizziness, perceptual distortions, hallucinations, tinnitus;
  - slurred speech, ataxia, nystagmus, tremor, hyporeflexia, muscle weakness.
- *Harmful effects:*
  - inhalation of vomit, asphyxiation, stupor, death;
  - fatal accidents.

Benzodiazepines

See the section on pharmacology.

Schizophrenia, schizotypal and delusional disorders

Schizophrenia

Epidemiology

- Equal sex distribution.
- Younger age of onset in males.
- Lifetime risk approx. 1%.
- More common in:
  - urban areas;
  - lower social classes (? cause or effect).

Clinical features

Appearance and behaviour:
- Insidious onset of social withdrawal and personality deterioration.
- Inactivity, loss of initiative and motivation.
- Self-neglect, odd behaviour, laughing for no reason.
- Catatonic symptoms (rare) – excitement, posturing, waxy flexibility, negativism, mutism, stupor, command automatism.

Mood:
- Depression and anxiety in early stages.
- Perplexity.
- Flattening or blunting of affect, inappropriate/incongruous affect.

Speech:
- Demonstrates underlying thought disorder.
- Use of odd words – neologisms, word salad.

Thought:
- Preoccupied with own thoughts, concrete thinking.
- Loosening of associations; nonsensical, tangential thinking.
- Stream of thought may be pressured or slowed, disturbed by thought blocking or withdrawal.
- Delusions – primary or secondary, one or systematised; delusional perception.*
- Persecutory delusions are most common, also delusions of reference, grandiosity, nihilism.
- Delusions of alien control of thoughts (withdrawal, insertion, broadcasting), actions, will, mood and somatic functions.*

Perception:
- Auditory hallucinations are the most common:
  - voices giving running commentary;*
  - voices discussing patient in the third person;*
  - hearing thoughts spoken aloud;*
  - second person command hallucinations can also occur;
  - often critical or frightening in content, usually of the same quality as hearing real voices.
- Olfactory, tactile, somatic and visual hallucinations can occur.

Cognition:
- Orientated.
- Impaired attention and concentration may result in memory impairment.

Insight:
- Usually impaired.
- Risk of violence and non-compliance with treatment.

Signs:
- May have abnormal involuntary movements – tics, twitches, tardive dyskinesia.
- Dyspraxia, agnosia.
- Soft signs – non-specific, non-localised neurological findings.

Presentation in the elderly:
- Delusional ideas, usually well-organised and persecutory in nature.

---

*Identifies Schneider's First Rank Symptoms.

- May show bizarre behaviour, self-neglect, may complain to police about neighbours.
- Thought disorder not as prominent.
- Hallucinations are mainly auditory.
- Personality preserved.
- Associated with deafness, social isolation, organic brain disease.

Classification (ICD10)

A diagnosis of schizophrenia requires one or more symptoms from group (a) or at least 2 from group (b). Symptoms should last for at least one month.

Group (a):
1. Thought echo, thought insertion, thought withdrawal, thought broadcasting.
2. Delusional perception; delusions of control, influence or passivity clearly referred to body movements or specific thoughts, actions or perceptions.
3. Auditory hallucinations:
   - running commentary on patient's behaviour;
   - discussing patient among themselves;
   - voices coming from some part of the body.
4. Persistent delusions of other types.

Group (b):
1. Hallucinations in any modality accompanied by delusions.
2. Incoherent or irrelevant speech:
   - neologisms;
   - breaks or interpolations in the train of thought.
3. Catatonic behaviour.
4. Negative symptoms:
   - apathy;
   - paucity of speech;
   - blunting or incongruity of affect;
   - under-activity, lack of initiative.

Schizophrenia may be further divided into subgroups depending on the most prominent symptoms:

Paranoid – fairly stable, often paranoid delusions and auditory hallucinations. Disturbances of mood, volition, speech, or catatonic symptoms are not prominent.

Hebephrenic – affective changes are prominent, behaviour may be irresponsible and unpredictable. Disorganised thought and incoherent speech. Hallucinations and delusions do not dominate the picture.
Catatonic – psychomotor disturbances which may alternate between extremes.
Simple – slow, progressive development of behavioural change, negative symptoms and decline in functioning without being preceded by clear psychotic symptoms.

Investigations

- Urine drug screen.
- EEG – may show asymmetrical slow waves, sharp waves and spikes particularly on the left side; also exclude TLE.
- CT/MRI – cortical atrophy, increased ventricular volume, reduced volume of temporal lobes.
- Functional imaging – reduced blood flow in frontal regions (hypofrontality).
- Neuropsychological testing – may show problems with attention, verbal memory, learning, visuomotor processing.

Aetiology
Genetics:
- Family studies – increased rates in family members.
- Twin studies – greater concordance with monozygotic than dizygotic twins.
- Adoption studies – increased incidence of schizophrenia in the offspring of biological schizophrenic mothers.
- Mode of inheritance – unclear.

Neurodevelopmental hypothesis:
- Suggests that changes are present from an early age but become evident when the brain matures.
- Evidence of non-progressive abnormalities in the brain – enlarged ventricles and sulci; reduced volume of the temporal lobes; hypofrontality; abnormal EEG.

Perinatal factors:
- Winter birth excess – may be due to prenatal infection.
- Higher frequency of obstetric complications.

Biochemical:

- Dopamine hypothesis:
  - see the section on pharmacology;
  - antipsychotics block dopamine receptors; potency of blockade is proportional to effect;
  - amphetamines can increase dopamine levels and cause a schizo-phrenic-like picture;
  - isomers of flupentixol – only the isomer which binds to dopamine receptors has antipsychotic action.
- Serotonin:
  - some antipsychotic drugs block serotonin receptors;
  - LSD acts at serotonin receptors and can produce psychotic symptoms.
- Glutamate – phencyclidine binds with NMDA receptors and produces psychotic symptoms.

Psychosocial factors:

- Social maladjustment evident at an early stage of development especially in boys.
- Increased incidence of abnormal premorbid personalities particularly schizoid.
- Life events:
  - twice the risk of developing schizophrenia in the 6 months after a life event;
  - higher incidence of events before the onset of acute psychotic symptoms.
- Environmental factors:
  - amount of stimulation – over-stimulation can cause relapse of psychotic symptoms; under-stimulation can result in a poverty syndrome;
  - expressed emotion – high levels can cause relapse.

Schizotypal disorder

Clinical features

- No definite onset.
- Evolution and course like that of a personality disorder.
- Odd, eccentric or peculiar behaviour.
- Poor rapport, social withdrawal.
- Cold and aloof affect.
- Odd beliefs or magical thinking.

- Suspiciousness or paranoid ideas.
- Obsessive ruminations – dysmorphophobic, sexual or aggressive content.
- Unusual perceptual experiences.
- Transient quasipsychotic episodes.

Persistent delusional disorders

Epidemiology

- Equal sex distribution.
- Later age of onset.
- Higher in unmarried or divorced people, associated with interpersonal difficulties.

Clinical features

- Single delusion or set of related delusions.
- Usually persistent and sometimes lifelong.
- Not classified as schizophrenic, affective or organic.
- No persistent hallucinations.
- Personality preserved.

Specific types of delusional disorder

- Pathological jealousy – delusion that partner is being unfaithful.
- De Clerambault's syndrome – usually a woman believing (wrongly) that a man, usually of higher social status, is in love with her.
- Cotard's syndrome – extreme nihilistic hypochondriacal delusions.
- Capgras syndrome – delusion that a known person has been replaced by an exact double.
- Frégoli syndrome – delusion that a number of people are a single persecutor in disguise.
- Induced psychosis (folie à deux) – dominant person with fixed delusions appears to induce similar delusions in a suggestible partner.

Schizoaffective disorder

Clinical features

- Sudden onset, good premorbid functioning.
- Both affective and schizophrenic symptoms are prominent, but do not justify a diagnosis of either schizophrenia or depressive or manic episodes.
- Define type of episode as manic, depressive or mixed.

Affective disorders

Depression

Epidemiology

- Very common, point prevalence of symptoms 13–20%.
- More common in
  - women (F:M = 2:1);
  - widowed/divorced people;
  - urban areas;
  - lower social classes;
  - unemployed.
- Often begins in late twenties or early thirties.

Clinical features

Appearance and behaviour:
- Appear miserable, downturned mouth, furrowed brow, tearful, worried.
- Hunched posture, look at floor.
- May exhibit evidence of self-neglect, weight loss, self-harm.
- Psychomotor retardation or agitation.

Mood:
- Low mood – more severe and longer lasting than ordinary unhappiness.
- Lose reactivity of mood – no improvement with good news, etc.
- Diurnal mood variation (DMV) – characteristically worse in the morning.
- May be anxious or irritable.

Thoughts:
- Negative thoughts about:

  past – guilt, blame;

  present – low self esteem, feel a failure, see the unhappy side, helplessness;

  future – hopelessness, expects failure and for bad things to happen.
- Suicidal ideation.
- Hypochondriacal ideas, obsessive compulsive symptoms.
- Delusions – guilt, worthlessness, ill health, nihilistic, persecutory, poverty, Cotard's syndrome.

Perception:
- Visual distortions, pseudohallucinations.
- Auditory hallucinations – 2nd person, command, mood congruent.
- Hallucinations in other modalities.
- Derealisation, depersonalisation.

Cognition:
- Poor attention and concentration which leads to poor memory.

Biological features:
- Poor appetite, weight loss, constipation, reduced energy.
- Loss of libido.
- Sleep disturbance – initial insomnia, early morning waking (EMW), frequent waking.

Social features:
- Marital discord.
- Alcohol misuse.
- Unemployment, financial difficulties.

Atypical presentations:
- Reversal of biological symptoms – weight gain, bingeing, hypersomnia with an inverted sleep pattern.
- Incongruent psychotic symptoms.
- Masked depression – low mood is not the main feature.
- Stupor – fully conscious but motionless and mute.

Presentation in the elderly:
- Agitation more frequent than retardation.
- Behavioural disturbance.
- Histrionic behaviour, hypochondriacal preoccupations.
- Paranoia, delusions.
- Pseudodementia.

Classification (ICD10)

Depressive episodes – symptoms lasting 2 weeks or more:

Mild – at least 4 symptoms [2 from (a)].
Moderate – at least 6 symptoms [2 from (a)].
Severe – at least 8 symptoms [all 3 from (a)].
   Group (a):
   low mood;
   low energy;
   loss of interest/pleasure.
   Group (b):

low self-confidence/self-esteem;
guilt/self reproach;
suicidal ideas/behaviour;
sleep disturbance;
poor concentration;
change in appetite/weight;
change in psychomotor activity.
Mild or moderate depressive episodes may also have a somatic syndrome with 4 symptoms from:
loss of appetite;
loss of weight (> 5%);
loss of libido;
EMW;
DMV;
psychomotor agitation/retardation;
loss of interest/pleasure;
loss of emotional reactivity.
Further classification of severe depression:
are psychotic symptoms present?
are the psychotic symptoms mood congruent or incongruent?

Recurrent depressive disorder

- At least one previous episode lasting > 2 weeks.
- 2 months between episodes without significant mood symptoms.
- Specify type of current episode or status.

Investigations

- Rating scales – Beck Depression Inventory, Hamilton Depression Rating Scale, Montgomery–Asperg Depression Rating Scale.
- Physical investigations; e.g., blood tests to exclude possible organic causes.

Aetiology

Genetics:
- Family studies – first degree relatives have increased risk.
- Twin studies – greater concordance for monozygotic than for dizygotic twins.
- Adoption studies – higher rate of depression in adoptees whose biological parents have affective illness.

Neurotransmitters:
- There is evidence that abnormality in neurotransmitters causes depression.
- Serotonin:
  - tryptophan (a precursor of serotonin) levels are reduced in depressed patients and L-tryptophan is a weak antidepressant;
  - 5HIAA, a metabolite of serotonin, is reduced in depressed patients;
  - antidepressants that increase serotonin relieve depression;
  - abnormalities in platelet serotonin in depressed patients – reduced uptake and increased receptor binding.
- Noradrenaline:
  - changes in receptor binding and numbers;
  - suicides show increased beta-adrenergic receptors at post-mortem.
- Dopamine
  - HVA level (measure of dopamine turnover) in CSF of depressed patients is low;
  - drugs that increase dopamine levels can elevate mood;
  - ECT may work by affecting dopamine function.

Neuroendocrine:
- Cortisol secretion is increased and some depressed patients show non-suppression on the Dexamethasone Suppression Test.
- Thyroid hormones are affected with a blunted TSH response to TRH.
- Tri-iodothyronin augmentation may increase the benefit of anti-depressants.

Organic causes:
- Physical illness may act as a life event precipitating a depressive episode or may be a direct cause of depression:
- Drugs – neuroleptics, anticonvulsants, steroids, L-dopa, antihypertensives.
- Neurological disorders – MS, CVA, Parkinson's disease, dementia.
- Endocrine disorders – thyroid disorder, Addison's disease, Cushing's syndrome, hypopituitarism, hyperparathyroidism, diabetes mellitus.
- Infections – influenza, infectious mononucleosis, hepatitis A, brucellosis.
- Other – SLE, carcinoma, anaemia.

Psychosocial:
- Life events are recent major changes in the social environment. Paykel reported that depressives had 3 times as many life events in the 6 months prior to a depressive episode. The relative risk of developing

depression is increased 6 times in the 6 months following a threatening life event.
- Brown and Harris described long-term difficulties and vulnerability factors.
  Long-term difficulties are prolonged stressful circumstances that may cause depression over a period of time and add to the effects of life events. Vulnerability factors do not cause depression directly but increase the effects of life events.
  Vulnerability factors include: lack of a confidant; no work outside the home; 3 or more children under the age of 14 at home; loss of mother before age 11.
- Expressed emotion – there is a link between high EE and the onset and risk of relapse of depression particularly when critical remarks are involved.
- Other theories – parental discord, childhood abuse, neurotic personality.

Cognitive theories:
- Learned helplessness – described by Seligman, who demonstrated that animals which experienced unpleasant situations they could not control or escape from, later failed to learn to avoid escapable stimuli in similar situations and showed signs of depression, e.g. disturbed sleep, poor appetite.
- Helplessness in humans can lead to motivational, cognitive and emotional deficits.
- Beck proposed a model of negative views of self, world and future. These views were perpetuated by:
  – depressive underlying beliefs;
  – negative automatic thoughts;
  – errors in reasoning.
- Other behavioural models:
  Lewinsohn – reduced frequency of social reinforcement.
  Ferster – loss of reinforcible behaviour.
  Rehm – deficits in self-monitoring, self-evaluation, and self-reinforcement.
- Bibring and Jacobson suggested the role of loss of self-esteem.

Psychoanalytic theories:
- Freud – proposed the loss of an object towards which ambivalent feelings are felt; loss results in despair and the negative feelings towards the object are redirected at the self.
- Klein – proposed a failure to pass through the 'depressive position'.

Dysthymia

Clinical features

- Chronic depression of mood not sufficiently severe for a diagnosis of depressive disorder.
- Lasts at least several years.
- At least 3 of the following symptoms occur during some of the periods of depression:
  Reduced energy/activity.
  Insomnia.
  Loss of self-confidence.
  Difficulty in concentrating.
  Frequent tearfulness.
  Loss of interest in pleasurable activities.
  Hopelessness or despair.
  Perceived inability to cope.
  Pessimism about the future.
  Social withdrawal.
  Reduced talkativeness.

Mania

Epidemiology

- Equal sex distribution.
- Often begins in mid-twenties.
- More common in:
  - urban areas;
  - higher social classes;
  - divorced people (? consequence of illness).

Clinical features

Appearance and behaviour:
- Bright coloured clothing in unusual combinations, may be untidy, lots of make-up.
- Excessive gesture, over-active, difficulty in remaining seated.
- Over-familiar, disinhibited.
- May be abusive with a risk of assault.
- Manic stupor – rare; fully conscious, mute, immobile, state of elation.

Speech:
- Outspoken.
- Talk excessively at a fast rate, difficult to interrupt.
- Pressure of speech.

Mood:
- Cheerful, elated or irritable.
- Infectious gaiety, excitable.
- Mood swings/labile.

Thoughts:
- Racing thoughts or flight of ideas.
- Inflated self-esteem.
- Optimistic.
- Expansive ideas, over-estimate abilities/wealth/status.
- Delusions – usually grandiose or persecutory, can be of reference or passivity.

Perception:
- Auditory hallucinations – usually mood congruent, may talk to the person about their special abilities.
- Occasional visual hallucinations.

Cognition:
- Distractible, may appear forgetful.

Insight:
- Usually no insight.

Physical features:
- Reduced sleep – wake early but feel full of energy.
- Increased appetite.
- Increased libido.

Social features:
- Over-spending, debts, loss of job.
- Sexual indiscretions.

Presentation in the elderly:
- Similar to younger people.
- More common symptoms include – surliness, garrulousness, mixed affective states, slowed flight of ideas, cognitive impairment.

Classification (ICD10)

Hypomania: Elevated/irritable mood for at least 4 days with at least 3 symptoms from below. There may be considerable interference with work or social activity:

1. Increased activity/restlessness:
2. Increased talkativeness.
3. Increased sexual energy.
4. Over-familiarity.
5. Over-spending.
6. Reduced sleep
7. Reduced concentration.

Manic episode: Elevated/irritable mood for at least a week, severe enough to disrupt ordinary work and social activities more or less completely, plus at least 3 symptoms from:

1. Increased activity/restlessness.
2. Increased talkativeness/pressure of speech.
3. Increased self-esteem/grandiosity.
4. Racing thoughts/flight of ideas.
5. Reduced sleep.
6. Reckless behaviour.
7. Distractible.
8. Disinhibition.
9. Marked sexual energy/indiscretions.

Further classification of manic episode:
- Are psychotic symptoms present?
- Are they mood congruent or incongruent?

Bipolar affective disorder:
- Two or more episodes of disturbed mood and activity.
- Recurrent hypomania/mania or depression and hypomania/mania.
- Specify type of current episode/state.

Rapid cycling disorder: Characterised by four or more episodes in one year.

Investigations

- Investigations to exclude possible organic causes.
- Urine drug screen.
- CT/MRI if localised neurological signs.

Aetiology

Genetics:
- Family studies – increased risk of bipolar and unipolar mood disorder in first degree relatives.

- Twin studies – greater concordance with monozygotic twins. Twins reared apart show concordance which suggests genetic rather than environmental effects.
- Adoption studies – higher incidence of mood disorder in adoptees with affected biological parents.

Organic causes:

- Insomnia/sleep deprivation – may precipitate a manic episode.
- Childbirth.
- Drugs may trigger mania:
  - psychostimulants – amphetamines, cocaine;
  - dopamine agonists – L-dopa;
  - anticholinergics;
  - steroids;
  - antidepressants, especially SSRI's (Important trigger of rapid cycling disorder).
- Physical illnesses:
  Endocrine – thyrotoxicosis, Cushing's disease;
  Brain disease – frontal lobe damage, head injury, tumours, epilepsy, MS, cerebrovascular disease, dementia.
- Neurotransmitters – excess of monoamines.

Social:

- Life events – may precipitate episodes of mania particularly the first episode.
- High expressed emotion – increases the risk of relapse.

Cyclothymia

Clinical features

- Persistent instability of mood involving numerous periods of depression and mild elation.
- Not severe or prolonged enough for diagnosis of bipolar affective disorder or recurrent depressive disorder.
- At least 3 of the symptoms listed under dysthymia should be present during some of the periods of depression.
- At least 3 of the following symptoms should be present during some of the periods of mood elevation:
  1. Increased energy/activity.
  2. Decreased need for sleep.
  3. Inflated self-esteem.

4. Creative thinking.
5. Gregariousness.
6. Increased talkativeness or wittiness.
7. Increased interest in pleasurable activities.
8. Over-optimism or exaggeration of past achievements.

Suicide and non-fatal deliberate self-harm

Suicide

Epidemiology

- Suicide accounts for approximately 1% of all deaths.
- True figure unclear because coroner verdicts report suicide only if there is clear evidence of suicidal intent.
- Methods used include:
  - overdose (half of female suicides, a third of male suicides);
  - carbon monoxide poisoning (half of male suicides);
  - hanging, shooting, drowning, jumping from high buildings.
- More common in:
  - males;
  - older age;
  - urban areas;
  - people living alone – divorcees/widowers/widows.
  - social classes I and V;
  - prisoners;
  - spring and summer;
  - eastern and northern European countries;
  - certain professions – vets, farmers, doctors, pharmacists;
  - people with chronic physical illnesses and chronic pain.

Aetiology

- Durkheim proposed four types of suicide:
  1. *Egotistic* – poor integration into society due to behaviour of the individual.
  2. *Anomic* – loosened bonds between people in society, no norms regulating behaviour.
  3. *Altruistic* – over-integration into society.

4. *Fatalistic* – excessive regulation by society so that the individual has no personal freedom/hope.

- Suicide tends to cluster in families.
- Imitation may precipitate some cases.
- Life events are more common prior to suicide.
- Abnormal neurochemistry – low levels of serotonin and 5HIAA found in post-mortem brain studies.
- Psychiatric illness:

  Depression – 15% eventually commit suicide, higher risk with insomnia, memory problems, self-neglect, delusions and retardation.

  Alcohol dependence – 15% commit suicide.

  Personality disorder – 10% commit suicide.

  Schizophrenia – up to 10% may eventually commit suicide.

Non-fatal deliberate self-harm

Epidemiology

- Common admissions to acute medical wards.
- Actual prevalence unclear as not all cases will present to hospitals/clinics.
- Methods include:
  - overdose (majority of cases);
  - self-laceration.
- Commonly associated with alcohol – up to 40% of cases.
- Risk of repetition – 15–20% in the year after the act.
- 10% eventually commit suicide.
- More common in:
  - females;
  - younger age group;
  - lower social class, over-crowded accommodation, social mobility;
  - divorcees;
  - unemployed.
- Features of deliberate self-laceration:
  - irritability and increasing tension;
  - relief after the act – sight of blood is often important;
  - sometimes experience shame and disgust afterwards.

Aetiology

- Triggers:
  - quarrel;

- separation/rejection;
- illness;
- court appearance.
• Personality disorder – particularly borderline and dissocial types.
• Alcohol dependence.
• Early parental loss, neglect or abuse.
• Biochemical basis:
  - low levels of 5HIAA in CSF of psychiatric patients with a history of self-harm;
  - a specific type of self-injurious behaviour is associated with Lesch Nyhan syndrome that has an underlying, inherited abnormality of uric acid metabolism.

Neurotic, stress-related and somatoform disorders

Anxiety disorders

A group of abnormal states that are characterised by the mental and physical features of anxiety. These can be divided into:

• Generalised anxiety disorder.
• Panic disorder.
• Phobias:
  - agoraphobia;
  - social phobia;
  - specific phobias.

Generalised anxiety disorder

Epidemiology

• More common in females.
• One year prevalence 2.5–6.4%.

Clinical features and classification (ICD-10)

Anxiety is persistent and not limited to any particular circumstances. At least 6 months of tension, worry and apprehension.

At least 4 symptoms from below [at least one from (1)]:

1. *Autonomic arousal*
   - palpitations/tachycardia;
   - sweating;
   - trembling or shaking;
   - dry mouth.
2. *Chest/abdomen*
   - difficulty in breathing, choking feeling, chest pain or discomfort;
   - nausea or abdominal distress.
3. *Mental state*
   - dizzy/unsteady/faint/light-headed feeling;
   - derealisation, depersonalisation;
   - fear of dying;
   - fear of losing control, going crazy or passing out.
4. *General*
   - hot/cold flushes, numbness/tingling, muscle tension/aches/pains;
   - restlessness and inability to relax, feeling on edge;
   - lump in throat or difficulty in swallowing.
5. *Non-specific*
   - easily startled, difficulty in concentrating, persistent irritability;
   - initial insomnia due to worry.

Aetiology

Genetics
- Family studies – increased rates of anxiety disorders, particularly in female relatives.
- Twin studies – suggest some genetic contribution due to greater concordance between monozygotic twins. Heritability of about 30%.

Psychological:
- Conditioning – excessive lability of the autonomic nervous system and generalisation of fear to normal neutral stimuli.
- Psychoanalytic – anxiety is caused by intrapsychic conflicts.

Premorbid personality – may be normal; or may be associated with anxious and anankastic personality disorders.

Early experiences – poor parenting, separation, childhood abuse.

Stressful events – particularly those that are threatening may precipitate anxiety disorder.

Panic disorder

Epidemiology

- Twice as common in females.
- Lifetime prevalence 1.4%.

Clinical features

- Several severe attacks of anxiety within a month.
- Unpredictable; not associated with any particular situation or object.
- Anticipatory anxiety develops, which may itself precipitate an attack.
- Characteristics of a panic attack:
  - discrete episode of intense fear and discomfort;
  - starts abruptly;
  - peaks within a few minutes and lasts at least some minutes;
  - at least 4 anxiety symptoms are present;
  - often a secondary fear of dying, losing control or going mad.

Aetiology

Genetics
- Increased risk of panic disorder in relatives.
- Increased risk of alcoholism in relatives.

Life events
- Increased number of life events in the year prior to onset, particularly if the events are an illness or the death of a relative.
- Fears of developing a serious illness may precipitate and reinforce symptoms of anxiety.

Physiological
- Association with reduced blood flow in the frontal lobes.
- A number of different substances can precipitate panic attacks; e.g. sodium lactate, flumazenil, CCK, caffeine.
- Drugs that effect serotonin receptors are used to treat panic disorder, e.g. SSRI's.
- Hypersensitive respiratory control system with increased carbon dioxide sensitivity.

Cognitive:
- Panic cycle – stimuli → perceived threat → apprehension and fear → bodily sensations → catastrophic processing of body symptoms → perceived threat, etc.

Phobias

Epidemiology

- More common in females, except social phobia which has an equal sex distribution.
- Prevalence: specific (simple) phobia > agoraphobia > social phobia.

Clinical features of phobias

- Same core symptoms as those of generalised anxiety disorder but symptoms occur only in certain circumstances.
- Fear is out of proportion to objective risk.
- Fear cannot be reasoned or explained away.
- Beyond voluntary control.
- Anticipatory anxiety.
- Leads to avoidance.

Aetiology of phobias

Genetic:
- Higher prevalence of phobias in families.
- Social phobia – three times the risk in relatives.

Psychological:
- Observational learning of other people, particularly parents.
- Classical conditioning:
  - an association made between a neutral stimulus and an unpleasant stimulus resulting in subsequent anxiety when the neutral stimulus is next encountered;
  - anxiety becomes generalised and associated with an increasing number of neutral situations.
- Operant conditioning – reduction of fear seen as a powerful reinforcer leading to persistence of a successful avoidance response.
- Preparedness theory – certain phobias may be innate, e.g. fear of animals or heights.
- Psychoanalytic – phobias represent a particular conflict and result in the avoidance of situations specific to that conflict.

Social:
- Life events may precipitate phobias.
- Perpetuated by over-protective family members.

Clinical features of different phobias

Agoraphobia:
- Fear and avoidance of:
  - crowds;
  - public places;
  - travelling alone;
  - travelling away from home.
- Symptoms of anxiety in the feared situation.
- Anticipatory anxiety of encountering the situation.
- Symptom severity may vary depending on circumstances, e.g. often less when with a family member.
- Increasing isolation and dependence on others.

Social phobia:
- Fear or avoidance of being the focus of attention or fear of behaving inappropriately.
- Fears occur in social situations:
  - speaking in public;
  - eating in public;
  - entering small group settings, e.g. parties, meetings.
- Symptoms of anxiety along with at least one of:
  - blushing or shaking;
  - fear of vomiting;
  - urgency or fear of micturition or defecation.
- Marked avoidance which may result in complete isolation.
- Association with alcohol abuse.

Specific (simple) phobias:
- Fear and avoidance of certain objects or in certain situations only:
  - creatures – insects, dogs;
  - natural occurrences – thunderstorms, water;
  - situations – claustrophobia, heights, flying;
  - blood, needles, hospitals, dentists.

Obsessive compulsive disorder

Epidemiology

- Begins in early adulthood.
- Lifetime prevalence 1.9–3.3%.
- Equal sex distribution.

Clinical features

- Obsessional thoughts, ideas, images or impulses that repeatedly enter the patient's mind in a stereotyped way.
- Compulsive acts or rituals or stereotyped behaviours that are regularly repeated, e.g. checking, counting and washing.
- Features:
  - originate in the mind of the patient;
  - repetitive and unpleasant;
  - patient tries to resist them;
  - the experience is not itself pleasurable.
- Cause distress or interfere with functioning.

Aetiology

Genetics
- Family studies – increased rate of psychiatric illness in relatives.
- Twin studies – suggest greater concordance with monozygotic twins but are not conclusive.
- Association between Tourette's syndrome, an inherited condition, and obsessive compulsive symptoms.

Neurotransmitters:
- Serotonin – role suggested due to the treatment effects of clomipramine that reduces the uptake of serotonin; it also has a weak effect on noradrenaline.
- Suggested serotonergic subsensitivity.
- Dopamine – an abnormality may be present in the dopaminergic system.

Brain injury:
- Abnormalities in the limbic system, basal ganglia and frontal lobe.
- Evidence of increased metabolic activity in fronto-orbital areas on PET scanning.
- Association with other disorders including encephalitis lethargica.

Premorbid personality – association with anankastic personality.

Psychological:
- Learned responses – the reduction in anxiety that occurs after the act/thought may reinforce the behaviour.
- Psychoanalytic – regression to anal stage of development, use defences of reaction formation and magical undoing.

Post-traumatic stress disorder

Epidemiology

- 25% of people experiencing a traumatic event develop PTSD.
- More common
  - in women;
  - in lower social classes;
  - when other psychiatric problems are present.
- Trauma should be
  - sudden with no time for psychological preparation;
  - exceptionally threatening or catastrophic in nature;
  - enough to cause a sense of helplessness and distress.

Clinical features

- *Re-experiencing trauma:*
  - intrusive memories – unwanted, short duration, triggered by minor stimuli;
  - flashbacks.
- *Avoidance behaviour:*
  - numbness, detachment, deny connection with the trauma;
  - reduced interest in activities, detachment from friends/family, isolation;
  - excessive pointless activity.
- Difficulty remembering stressful events at will.
- *Hyperarousal:*
  - increased startle responses;
  - poor concentration, sweating, trembling, fatigue;
  - sleep problems – initial insomnia, fear of nightmares.
- Lack of emotional responsiveness.
- Anxiety, irritability, depression, anger, fear.
- Ideas of self-harm, guilt, shame.
- Depersonalisation and dissociative states.

Aetiology

- Genetic – twin studies suggest that differences in susceptibility are partly genetic.
- Neurotransmitters – noradrenaline, dopamine, GABA and opioid systems may be involved.

- Personality predisposition – neuroticism.
- Disturbed early environment.
- Learned helplessness.

Adjustment disorders

Clinical features

- Distress and emotional disturbance arising within 1 month of a stressful life event.
- Individual predisposition/vulnerability is important.
- Manifestations include:
  - brief depressive reaction – duration less than 1 month;
  - prolonged depressive reaction – duration up to 2 years;
  - mixed anxiety and depressive reaction;
  - predominant disturbance of other emotions;
  - predominant disturbance of conduct;
  - mixed disturbance of emotions and conduct;
  - other specified predominant symptoms.

Dissociative disorders

Clinical features

- Partial or complete loss of normal integration between
  - memories of the past,
  - awareness of identity and immediate sensations, and
  - control of body movements.
- Marked denial of problems which are obvious to others.
- Tendency to remit after a few weeks or months.
- Associated with traumatic events, intolerable problems or interpersonal difficulties.
- Presumed to be psychogenic in origin.
- Symptoms often represent patient's idea of how the illness would appear.
- No evidence of physical disorder.

Types of dissociative disorder

- Dissociative amnesia.
- Dissociative fugue.

- Dissociative stupor.
- Trance and possession disorders.
- Dissociative motor disorders.
- Dissociative convulsions.
- Dissociative anaesthesia and sensory loss.
- Other dissociative disorders:
  - Ganser's syndrome;
  - multiple personality disorder.

Somatisation disorder

Epidemiology

- Prevalence of up to 0.5% in the UK.
- More common in:
  - females;
  - early adult life;
  - association with other psychiatric illnesses, e.g. depression.

Classification (ICD10)

1. At least 2 years of complaints of multiple and variable physical symptoms that cannot be explained by any detectable physical disorders.
2. Preoccupation with symptoms causing persistent distress. Repeated consultations with GP or hospital specialists.
3. Persistent refusal to accept reassurance that there is no adequate physical cause for the symptoms.
4. 6 or more of the following (in at least 2 groups):
   Gastrointestinal – abdominal pain, nausea, feeling bloated, bad taste/coated tongue, vomiting/regurgitation, frequent and loose bowel motions.
   Cardiovascular – breathlessness, chest pains.
   Genitourinary – dysuria/frequency, unpleasant feeling in genitals, vaginal discharge.
   Skin and pain – blotches/skin discolouration, pains in limbs/joints/extremities, numbness or tingling sensations.

Aetiology

Genetic:
- Greater monozygotic concordance.

- Association between female somatisers and dissocial behaviour and alcoholism in male relatives.
Environmental:
- Higher rates of parental illness.
- Higher rates of physical illness during childhood.
- Parental lack of care.

Hypochondriacal disorder

See the section on psychopathology.

Dysmorphophobia

See the section on psychopathology.

Eating disorders

Anorexia nervosa

Epidemiology

- Prevalence 1–2 per 1000 women.
- More common in:
  - females (F:M=10:1);
  - schoolgirls;
  - higher social classes;
  - models, dancers, gymnasts;
  - western countries.
- Onset at adolescence to early 20s

Clinical features

- Self-induced weight loss by:
  - self-induced vomiting;
  - self-induced purging;
  - excessive exercise;
  - misuse of diuretics, appetite suppressants.
- No pleasure from eating, enjoy cooking for others.
- Withdrawal, irritability, poor concentration, insomnia.

- Depressed mood.
- Thoughts:
  - morbid fear of fatness;
  - distorted body image;
  - denial of the problem;
  - fear of losing control of eating;
  - preoccupation with thoughts of food;
  - possible ideation of suicide.

Classification (ICD10)

1. Body weight 15% below normal or expected weight.
2. Self-induced weight loss.
3. Self-perception of being too fat, with an intrusive fear of fatness.
4. Endocrine disorder – amenorrhoea or delayed puberty or prepubertal onset.

Physical signs and complications of starvation

General – emaciation, lanugo hair.
Cardiovascular – bradycardia, hypotension, cardiac arrhythmias, heart failure, peripheral oedema.
Metabolic – slowed metabolic rate, dehydration, hypoglycaemia, hypothermia, cold intolerance.
Gastrointestinal – delayed gastric emptying, constipation, pancreatitis, abnormal liver function.
Genitourinary – amenorrhoea, reduced libido, abnormal renal function, kidney stones.
Musculoskeletal – muscle wasting, osteoporosis.
Neurological – fits.

Investigations

- Weight, height, BMI (body mass index).
- Food diary.
- Physical status – looking for signs of starvation listed above.
- Blood tests:
  FBC – normochromic normocytic anaemia, leucopenia;
  U&E – ↓ potassium, signs of dehydration;
  TFT – ↓ T4;
  LFT – ↑ AST, alkaline phosphatase, gamma-GT;

Hormones – ↑ growth hormone; ↓ LH, FSH, oestrogen;
Others – ↓ glucose, Mg, zinc, phosphate; ↑ amylase, cholesterol, cortisol.
• Eating Disorder Examination – structured interview.
• Eating Attitudes Test – self-report questionnaire.

Aetiology

Genetic:
• Increased incidence of eating disorders in relatives.
• Twin studies – higher concordance for monozygotic twins.
• Increased risk of mood disorders in primary relatives.
Environmental:
• Cultural ideas and fashion images of being thin.
• Higher rates of physical illness in childhood.
• Higher rates of childhood sexual abuse.
• Family patterns of enmeshment and over-protection.
• Personality – higher prevalence of personality disorders.
Neurotransmitters:
• Serotonin – may modulate appetite and affect neuroendocrine function.
Psychological:
• Conditioning – physical changes at puberty may lead to phobic avoidance of food.
• Psychodynamic – oral stage of psychosexual development, fear of adulthood.

Bulimia nervosa

Epidemiology

• More common in females (F:M=10:1).
• Older age of onset than anorexia.
• Prevalence may increase with time.

Clinical features

• Weight may be low, normal or high.
• Bingeing followed by behaviours to counteract weight gain.
• Anxiety, irritability, depression, poor concentration.
• Thoughts:
  – morbid fear of fatness;
  – distorted body image;

- guilt and disgust after binges;
- possible suicidal ideation.
• Greater insight than patients with anorexia.

Classification (ICD10)

1. Recurrent episodes of over-eating (bingeing), at least twice a week for 3 months. Strong desire or compulsion to eat.
2. Attempts to counteract effects of food by one or more of:
   - self-induced vomiting;
   - self-induced purging;
   - alternating periods of starvation;
   - use of appetite suppressants, thyroid preparations or diuretics.
3. Intrusive dread of fatness.

Physical signs and complications

Gastrointestinal – eroded tooth enamel, enlarged salivary glands, diarrhoea, constipation, rectal prolapse.
Other – hard skin on knuckles, conjunctival haemorrhages; menstrual abnormalities.

Investigations

• Similar to anorexia nervosa.
• Blood tests:
  ↓ potassium, chloride, magnesium;
  ↑ amylase, bicarbonate.

Aetiology

Genetics:
• Higher concordance for monozygotic twins.
Physiological:
• Serotonin
  - mediates satiety;
  - 5HT-1C receptor sensitivity may be altered.
• Rigid dieting may precipitate episodes.
Psychological:
• Higher rates of personality difficulties.
• Low self-esteem.
• Higher rates of childhood sexual abuse.
• Higher rates of major depression, alcohol abuse and social phobia.

Personality disorders

Behaviour patterns which

- are deeply ingrained and enduring;
- appear as inflexible responses to a wide range of situations;
- result from developmental conditions;
- appear from late childhood or adolescence;
- continue into adulthood.

Clinical features of personality disorder

- Deviation of patterns of behaviour from expected and accepted norms.
- Deviations pervasive across a broad range of personal and social situations and in more than one of the following:
  - cognition;
  - affectivity;
  - control over impulses and gratification of needs;
  - way of relating to others.
- Distress to the person or adverse effects on society.
- Behaviour not due to other psychiatric or physical disorders.

Some features of specific personality disorders

Paranoid

Self-referential attitude.
Conspiratorial explanations of events.
Argumentative.
Refusal to forgive insults, bearing grudges.
Excess sensitivity to setbacks/rebuffs.
Suspiciousness, e.g. ideas regarding fidelity of partner.

Schizoid

Fantasise excessively.
Activities bring little pleasure.
No close relationships.
Trouble expressing feelings.
Affect cold.

Solitary activities.
Insensitive to social norms and conventions.

Dissocial

Callous unconcern for feelings of others.
Offer plausible rationalisations for behaviour.
No guilt.
Violent.
Irresponsible.
Cannot maintain relationships.
Tolerate little frustration.

Emotionally unstable

1) *Impulsive type:*
   Mood unstable.
   Argumentative.
   Violent/angry outbursts.
   Act unexpectedly.
   Rewards needed immediately.
   Impulsive.
   Consequences not considered.
2) *Borderline type:*
   Lack of control of anger.
   Unstable relationships.
   Chronic feelings of emptiness.
   Recurrent threats/acts of DSH.
   A lack of personal identity.
   Transient stress related psychotic symptoms.
   Impulsive.
   Variable moods.
   Efforts to avoid abandonment.

Histrionic

Dramatisation of self.
Readily bored.
Affect shallow and labile.
Must be centre of attention.
Attention seeking.
Theatricality.

Inappropriate seductiveness.
Continually seek excitement.
Suggestible.

Anankastic

Preoccupation with details/rules/schedules.
Excessive conscientiousness.
Doubt.
Adhere to social conventions.
Need for productivity.
Task completion problems due to perfectionism.
Inflexible.
Cautious.
Stubborn/rigid.

Anxious (avoidant)

Persistently anxious.
Avoid social situations.
Lifestyle restricted due to perceived need for security.
Expect to be criticised/rejected.
Socially inept (belief).

Dependent

Do not make life decisions.
Unduly compliant, and unwilling to make demands on others.
Lack self-reliance.
Loneliness feared.

Investigations

Personality questionnaires that can be presented:

• Eysenck Personality Inventory.
• Standardised Assessment of Personality.
• Personality Assessment Schedule.
• Millons Clinical Multiaxial Inventory.
• Disorder specific schedules, e.g. for borderline personality disorder.

Aetiology

General theories

- Aetiology largely unknown, probably the result of both genetics and environment.
- Heredity:
  - important for some personality disorders;
  - some personality traits are inheritable: introversion, depression, psychopathy and schizophrenia-like traits.
- Childhood experiences:
  - early attachments;
  - being a victim of violence and abuse;
  - pattern of parenting – over-protective and coercive parenting may cause problems;
  - certain childhood psychiatric disorders.
- Learning theory – modelling, influence of parents.

Theories specific to each disorder

- Paranoid
  - comorbidity with dissocial PD – may share similar early environmental risk factors;
  - projection of homosexual impulses;
  - feelings of inadequacy resulting in projection of hostility and rage onto others.
- Schizoid – presence of perinatal problems and developmental delay may suggest a neurodevelopmental disorder.
- Dissocial
  - association with family history of personality disorder;
  - twin studies – greater concordance with monozygotic twins;
  - adoption studies – higher incidence of criminality in biological parents of adoptees with dissocial personality;
  - adverse early environment – deprivation, abuse, prolonged institutional care;
  - association with conduct disorder, ADHD and aggressive temperament in childhood;
  - abnormal EEG findings with slow wave activity and spikes over temporal lobes.

- Borderline
  - adverse early environmental factors including lack of stable attachment during development, neglect, physical and sexual abuse;
  - higher incidence of personality disorder, psychiatric illness and marital difficulties in parents.
- Histrionic – difficulties in the Oedipal phase.
- Anankastic
  - obsessional traits, inheritable symptoms;
  - struggle for control with parents;
  - problems in the anal stage of sexual development.
- Anxious (avoidant) – often occurs with phobic disorder.
- Dependent
  - abnormal relationship patterns in the family – maternal overprotection.
  - fixation at oral stage of development.

Recommendations for further reading

General references

Gelder M, Gath D, Mayou R, Cowen P. Oxford Textbook of Psychiatry, 3rd edition. Oxford: Oxford University Press, 1996.

Johnstone E, Freeman C, Zealley AK. Companion to Psychiatric Studies, 6th edition. Edinburgh: Churchill Livingstone, 1998.

Psychology and human development

Gross RD. Psychology, A New Introduction. London: Hodder, 2000.

Atkinson RL. Introduction to Psychology. Harcourt Brace College Publishers, 1999.

Gupta DS and Gupta GM. Psychology for Psychiatrists. Whurr Publishers, 1999.

Munafo M. Psychology for the MRCPsych. Oxford: Butterworth Heinemann, 1998.

Psychopharmacology

British National Formulary (current edition).

Bazier S. Psychotropic Drug Directory 2000 – The Professionals' Pocket Handbook and Aide Memoire. Quay Books: Mark Allen Publishing, 2000.

Rang HP, Dale MM, Ritter JM. Pharmacology, 4th edition. Edinburgh: Churchill Livingstone, 1999.
Ritter JM, Lewis LD, Mant TGK. A Textbook of Clinical Pharmacology. London: Arnold, 2000.
Levi MI. Basic Notes in Psychopharmacology, 2nd edition. Petroc Press, 1997.

Psychopathology

Sims A. Symptoms in the Mind – An Introduction to Descriptive Psychopathology, 2nd edition. London: WB Saunders, 1999.
Bateman A and Holmes J. Introduction to Psychoanalysis: Contemporary Theory and Practice. Routledge, 1995.

Clinical

World Health Organisation. The ICD-10 Classification of Mental and Behavioural Disorders. Geneva: WHO, 1992.
World Health Organisation. Pocket Guide to the ICD-10 Classification of Mental and Behavioural Disorders With Glossary and Diagnostic Criteria for Research. Edinburgh: Churchill Livingstone, 1994 (in addition to general reference above).

Useful college publications

Stein G and Wilkinson G. Seminars in General Adult Psychiatry. Gaskell, 1998.
Chick J and Cantwell R. Seminars in Alcohol and Drug Misuse. Gaskell, 1998.
Butler R and Pitt B. Seminars in Old Age Psychiatry. Gaskell, 1998.